To Sarah, Hope this book will encourage, enjoy Carole

This Cruising Life
Book One

By

Carole and Ron May

Copyright Material

ISBN

978-0-9955724-0-9

Carole.sonadora2@gmail.com

This Crusing Life   Carole May

Preface

My name is Carole May I was a State registered Nurse, Clinical Nurse Tutor and my husband Ron was an electrical engineer contractor and we had been married for 6 years living in the very pretty little village of Raglan, Monmouthshire, where Ron had spent most of his life.

The sameness of everyday life had begun to get me down, we were in a rut. We decided we should do something about it. Deciding what was '**It**' was another matter.

Ron showed me a picture in a magazine he had been reading, it was open at a full page colour photograph of a yacht anchored just off a beautiful sandy bay with coconut palms in the background, and a lovely bronzed girl was emerging from the clear blue sea to join a handsome man sitting with his back against a palm tree.

It was difficult to imagine more of a contrast to the bleak scene through our living room window, rain, mist and cloud. It was a typical miserable, wet British November day. I looked at this lovely picture and said "This could be us! We are fit, young enough and have no-one else to consider, but ourselves." "There is just one thing wrong." said Ron.

"We haven't got a yacht and couldn't sail it if we did."

My reply to this was. "We could soon get one and it wouldn't take you long to learn how to sail it."

****

Apologies to the experienced yacht sailors, for having to explain a few yachting terms so that the non sailors, including Ron and myself can appreciate the joys of sailing.

Acknowledgements

I would like to thank the following people for their input and help with the formation of this book and to friends and neighbours who have helped and encouraged us in the build of Soñadora:

John Powell, Ron's long suffering apprentice electrician.

Joyce and Don Exton, neighbours.

Ken Evans for the use of his potato storage shed for the build of Soñadora.

Glyn and Shirley Powell, Bernard Thomas, for use of their heavy duty equipment ie Artic Lorry, JCB Drott and Crane.

Gwent Police Department for their escort.

Ray and wife Lyn original crew members.

Terry Compton, (Designer) Patrick Wentworth Boyd and his crew members, David Pelly, Bill Bullimore, Donald Westbury.

Newport container port staff.

Bob Graham, our very best Bristol Channel Pilot, who piloted Soñadora and her motley crew safely to Bristol.

Proof readers:- Eve Hart, David Dower and Peter Binder.

And a special thanks to Ron's brother Trevor, Pat and Peter their son for always being there when required and of course Mother May, a delightful Mother-in-law.

And an extra special thanks to Jean Jones, ICT Trainer who helped to transform our images and words into an enjoyable book format. Studio14, Island Road, Barry for Artwork advice.

Last but not least to all my good helpful friends in Barry and around the world.

To Soñadora, thank you for being so forgiving with your inexperienced crew, Ron and I, though we always felt safe at sea with you.

Finally, to Ron

Ron

Husband

My very best friend, lover and protector. Thank you for making our dreams come true with your quiet strength and self -confidence and the belief that despite our naivety we could cope with whatever the sea threw at us

I Love You

And Thank you Darling

xxxxxxxxxxxxxxxxxxx

Cheers! Come and Enjoy

Contents

"Carole, wake up." Ron said as he was shaking me awake. "Here is your tea. Bring it out on deck as we have visitors." I couldn't imagine who it could be as we had been at sea, out of sight of land for a week now. I stepped on deck into a beautiful morning. Our catamaran, Soñadora, was sailing quietly along. Then I saw them. Our first visitors since we had left Gibraltar were a pod of dolphins. They were leaping and playing, crossing and re-crossing our bows and speeding out from between our hulls. Dolphins are such happy creatures. Nature has given their faces a permanent smile. They were squeaking away at each other as they looked up at us from the clear blue-grey sea seeming to laugh at life and us funny humans.

This was the life we had been dreaming of for five years; the beginning of our first ocean crossing. We were just seven days out of Gibraltar nearing the Canary Islands which would be the first stopping place on our way to the Caribbean and the world.

It had all started one bleak November Saturday afternoon in the winter of 1969. In spite of the warmth from the log fire the cold and damp seemed to creep in everywhere. Looking out of the windows at the rain sodden countryside I thought, "What on earth are we doing here?" Only five years before I had been a Nursing Sister in sunny Queensland Australia.

I looked over at my husband Ron sitting comfortably in his favourite chair reading and looking the picture of contentment. I suddenly felt angry. "Is this what you intend to do for the rest of your life?" I growled at him. He looked up faintly puzzled at this unprovoked attack. "What's the matter?" "Did you park the car on your roses again?" he enquired. A reference to my erratic reversing the previous evening.

1

We had been married and living in the same lovely little village of Raglan, Monmouthshire in Wales for five years. Ron was an electrical contractor having lived most of his life in this area. I was a Clinical Nurse Tutor for the Gwent Health Authority based in St Woolos Hospital, Newport. This was the longest time I had lived in any one place since my mother died (age 41) when I was ten and the eldest of three. Two years later my father with his new wife, their one and two year old girls and we three (which brought us up to five - four girls and one boy) were off to my father's newest air force posting in Singapore. We lived in Changi for two years and then returned to the UK.

The sameness of everyday life had begun to get me down. "We are in a rut and we have got to do something about it," I replied. "Well, look at this then," he said passing the magazine he had been reading. It was open at a full-page colour photograph of a yacht anchored just off a beautiful, sandy golden bay with coconut palms in the background. A lovely bronzed girl was just emerging from the clear blue water to join a handsome man sitting with his back against a palm tree. It was difficult to imagine more of a contrast to the bleak scene through our living room window.

"This is just the thing," I said. "That could be us. We are fit, young enough and have no one else to consider but ourselves." "There is just one thing wrong," said Ron. "We haven't got a yacht and couldn't sail it if we had" I replied, "we could soon get one and it wouldn't take you long to learn to sail it!"

This joking conversation led into a serious discussion of the possibilities. We had no children, ties or responsibilities. Ron's mother was in her early 70's and very independent. His brother Trevor and his wife Pat lived only 100 yards away from her front door so they could handle any emergencies that arose.

As far as the actual sailing, we both could swim and were not bothered by being out of sight of land. Surprisingly a lot of very experienced yacht people do not like being far from the mainland.

Restless by nature, we had met on the liner HMT Empire Windrush bound for Australia. We were two of the many taking advantage of the £10 Pom Scheme that was available at that time (1959) sponsored by the Australian Government. The Scheme offered a fare of £10 if you stayed in Australia for two years. However, if you stayed less than two years you had to repay the fare in full.

We had met in the ship's ironing room. Ron was ironing a shirt and I was trying to press my first pair of long pants (making quite a mess of them). Ron looked over and suggested we swap. I quickly agreed. I pressed his shirt and he pressed my pants. What a perfect way to start a relationship.

When we docked at Sydney I was booked to go to Brisbane and Ron to stay in Sydney. We met from time to time while travelling and exploring Australia before returning to the UK in late 1963. We then married in October 1964.

Just talking about it cheered us up. We had each in our own way been unsettled for some time without telling the other. We decided there and then that come what may we must have a change. The London Boat Show was due soon and what better place to find out about yachts and the yachting world. We started to read all we could on the subject soon exhausting the local library.

January 1970 found us at the London Boat Show. Our hopes were high as we went through the turnstiles at the entrance. We walked around viewing the many different and beautiful monohull yachts. We selected the one we thought looked most suitable and went aboard. Though we had travelled on quite a few liners and cargo ships we had never actually been on board a small yacht. By now we had looked at many photographs and drawings of yacht interiors. It came as a great surprise to me to find out just how small the interior of this 35ft yacht was. It is amazing how a good photographer can double the apparent size of an interior. I quite upset the salesman by enquiring where he had hidden the rest of it! We quickly went to the largest yacht in the show and while it was much larger than the others it still fell far short of what we, in our ignorance, had imagined it would be.

We discussed our requirements with quite a few people at the show and they told us that to get the sort of accommodation we wanted would require a yacht in the 70ft range, much too large to be on display at the boat show. We did manage to get literature on the big Swans and Nicholsons however the price put them right out of our range. Back home we were quite depressed, and then cheered up when we realised there must be a second hand market. We could surely find something there.

We studied all the 'For Sale' advertisements in the yachting press. Weekends were spent visiting the likely possibilities. After two months there wasn't a rusting, rotting or sinking hulk within 200 miles we had not visited. We had noticed a yacht advertised in Malta that we thought might be the one, so April saw us there. The yacht turned out to be completely unsuitable!

Walking back along the quayside we got into conversation with a very nice chap sitting on the foredeck of his catamaran playing a guitar. After hearing our story he said, "What you want is a catamaran." He then invited us to come aboard his 30ft Oceanic catamaran for a look around. We had not considered the multihull yachts, knowing nothing about catamarans, as they were still relatively new on the market. We were very impressed with the spacious accommodation. The more we heard of his sailing experiences the more we realised this could perhaps be the answer to our problem. He invited us to join him, his wife and family of three children for a sail the following day to the Isle of Gozo. We

4

were surprised at the comfort and stability whilst sailing. It was possible to put a glass of gin and tonic on the deck without it moving. This delighted Ron! We found the lack of heel very agreeable (the heel is when a monohull yacht is blown over on its side to "spill" the wind i.e. prevent it from capsizing). We were fast learning the yachting language. He also brought to our attention the fact that he and his wife could sail this yacht with ease. The big monohulls we had been considering would need a crew to sail them. This was a point we hadn't really considered and was the last thing we would want.

Returning to England we investigated all aspects of multihulls viewing all the catamarans and trimarans available. We decided that of the two types we preferred the catamaran, although they are lumped together under the classification "multihulls" (catamarans have two hulls, trimarans have three) they are a totally different craft with very different sailing characteristics.

We heard horror stories of catamarans capsizing and breaking up due to people trying to turn racing cats (built light for speed) into ocean cruising catamarans (built for strength, comfort and carrying capacity). Back then you could not be certain to get the supplies needed, thus capacity was very important. It is different today as most islands have small well stocked supermarkets.

In 1971 we returned to the London Boat Show. The show-guide said there was a 42ft Solaris catamaran afloat and open for inspection at London Tower Bridge. We made a rapid move in that direction and saw the Solaris design for the first time. We went aboard and were delighted to find something very close to our ideal. It really was a superbly finished yacht inside and out with every aid and comfort one could think of.

The designer Terry Compton was aboard and listened with

real interest to our ideas. He suggested that the latest 48ft Solaris (which had just been successfully tank tested at Southampton University) would be more suitable for our requirements and regardless of its size could still be easily handled by the two of us and asked us if we would be interested in it.

Terry was quite surprised when Ron said he wanted to build it himself. Ron asked if it was possible for Terry and the Solaris shipyard to advise and give support during the build. Terry said he would be delighted and arranged to visit us in Raglan when the boat show was over. We came home very happy but wondered what we had really let ourselves in for, though confident that we could do it.

The first thing that Ron had to do to start the boat building process was to confirm, with his good friend Ken Evans that he could have the use of his potato shed for a couple of years. Ken owned a turkey farm where it was critical to keep the electricity supply and temperature at a certain level. With Ron on site, building the boat, he could closely monitor the levels, so Ken was more than happy for Ron to use the shed.

The potato shed had a great view of Raglan Castle which was the last castle to fall to Oliver Cromwell during the English Civil War (1646). So like Oliver Cromwell, the Mays were about to start their own battle to build the boat on Monday May 3rd 1971.

Back at work that Monday, I was constantly thinking about Ron. There are many trials and tribulations to building boats. Luckily we were happily oblivious to all of them but, reality was beginning to set in. Ron still had a business to run and I had to keep working. Money was not growing on our trees.

On leaving work I rushed straight to the farm to see how things were progressing. Fortunately, Ron had John his apprentice electrician to help him. It took them a week to chase the rats and field mice out of the shed and turn it into a clean, dry, warm and efficient workshop.

At last the weekend arrived and I could spend it helping Ron. The weather was lovely and sunny which added to the pleasure we both felt at actually beginning to make our dream come true. During that weekend, Ron had discovered that some sparrows had built a nest in the rafters and it would have to be removed, so I climbed the 12 ft. ladder, looked into the nest and found one stale egg. I was glad there were no chicks expecting me to feed them. Both egg and nest went into the bin. Later that year when the shed was a hive of activity the sparrows came back building another nest at the top corner of the shed door causing no problems. We also had the company of a little dog belonging to Avril (Ken's wife). He was a happy friendly fellow who obviously loved the farm and our company.

Following Terry's design plans of the Yacht to be, Ron had used conduit pipe which was easy to bend and weld into the desired Hull shapes, before screwing them onto the longitudinal wooden batons used as braces to hold them into position. All upside down of course (picture 1). Ron then warmed the airtex foam, shaped it and nailed it to the batons (picture 2) followed by sealing the foam with resin.

Terry had promised to show Ron how fibreglass was applied, so we had a very enjoyable two days with Terry and the

Solaris boat yard team in Southampton seeing a Solaris catamaran being fibreglassed.

On our return following Terry's design John and Ron, spent a very sticky three weeks applying the fibreglass and resin coatings. During this time Ron discovered he had a really bad phobia about getting sticky. He had to fight it every time he had to apply another resin coat. He also suffered from hay fever. He was not a happy bunny during this time. We (John and I) felt so sorry for him and did what we could to help.

Once the fibreglass coating was complete (first two pictures), the mould was taken outside, craned over to the right side up then taken back into the shed where it was stripped of all the wooden batons and conduit pipe frames, and then fibreglass and resin were applied to the inside over the foam using the same method as the outside, thus making it a male mould. A very strong build.

Once the inside of the hulls had been fibreglassed, the hulls were then taken out of the shed and stored around the back of it, so that there would be room to construct the top deck inside in the dry. The top deck was constructed in the same way as the hulls, only using end grain Balsa wood instead of the Airtex foam as this was lighter but just as strong.

The hulls parked behind the shed sat on a thick growth of grass. This proved to be fortunate, as Ron got into the habit of falling off the hulls (a drop of 15ft). His injuries could have been worse. He only fractured his ankle the first time, then almost to the day the following year he fell off again fracturing his wrist.

We began to look upon this as his annual break. I assured him he did not have to go to those lengths to get a holiday. I was concerned that the damage was creeping up his body so the last year of the build, became a race against time to g get it into the water, so that he could fall off it into the sea and not break his neck.

First stage of construction, batons fixed onto conduit pipes to form the desired shape

The finished shaping of the hulls with fibreglass over the foam. Carole sat on upside down keel

Ken and Ron admiring Glyn's skill at turning the hull over and then backing it back into the shed 1974

Soñadora being returned to the shed

Soñadora behind the shed

Ron Taking shelter

We soon had another reason to press on with the build. In April 1974, Whitbread (the brewers) announced that they were organising a long distance ocean yacht race for multihulls. The start was to be from Portsmouth on November 1st 1975. The first leg of the race was to Key West Florida (which is the leg we would be taking part in) via the Azores a 4,550 nautical mile transatlantic crossing with three more legs to follow.

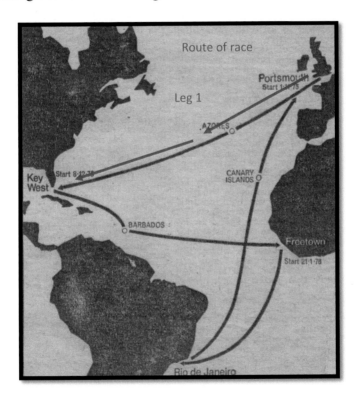

Multi-hulls prepare for 18,000 mile race 4 times crossing the Atlantic Ocean

It was reported that all together they were expecting 10 to 12 entries for the full 18,000 nautical mile race

Terry was very enthusiastic about the race, and persuaded Ron that it would be a very good experience for us to do the first leg. Within a week Terry had organised a crew of five very experienced Catamaran sailors including Patrick Wentworth Boyd, one of the world's most experienced yachtsmen. He was Chairman of the Multi Hull Ocean Cruising and Racing Association. He was to be our skipper and navigator! The rest of the crew were David Pelly, Bill Bullimore, Alan our Photographer and Terry Compton. Together they would teach us everything we needed to know about catamaran sailing.

As a new yacht we now had to get her registered with the British Ship Registry Department in Guernsey. This meant that we had to give it a name that would be unique to the yacht.

At that time I was attending Cardiff University which gave me access to their library. Ron promptly handed the job of finding a suitable name to me with the following instructions:

1. Single name only with no more than 7/8 letters

2. Easy to read /hear over the VHF

3. It meant something special to the three of us, (Ron, me and the yacht).

She had now definitely become an equal partner in our lives. I came away from the library with the name **Soñadora** Spanish for **"Dreamer."** We had honeymooned on the Island of Mallorca in the Mediterranean Sea. We loved the place and the people so it seemed natural to have a Spanish name. More importantly Ron liked it and it was accepted by the British Ship Registry.

Now that Soñadora was officially on the British Shipping Register she could be officially entered for the Whitbread Race. The entrance fee was paid and Soñadora was entered long before she was completed. She was an ocean cruiser not a racing catamaran, but we still had high hopes that she would put up a good performance.

To qualify for the race the yacht had to complete 1000 nautical miles off shore, under sail, carrying a specified number of crew, adequate water and stores for the first leg. Once completed she was to be inspected and approved by experts selected by the race committee to confirm her suitability for the race. All of this meant that we now had a completion date. Things became more urgent. Various changes were made to Soñadora to improve her performance. She was changed from a ketch to a sloop with the most drastic change being the out drive system which was to cause great problems for us in the time ahead.

By the end of March 1975 she was ready to be launched. Ron arranged for Soñadora to be launched at the Newport Container Shipping Port 16 miles away in mid April. This sounds simple but we had problems such as that she was too wide to get down the lane from the shed where she had been built. Our solution was to transport her on a large articulated lorry for half a mile across the field, taking down a council fence to get onto the main road; we then had to drive down the newly constructed main road to Newport.

We had jokingly told the villagers that the Department of Highways had kindly built the road especially for us. Of course they believed it!! Being a Sunday most of the villagers, friends and family had come to watch making bets that we would not make it. However they were happy when they lost. One of the village wags told a woman who had stopped to watch that we had built a latter day Noah's Ark to be ready for another great flood due at any moment! She was advised not to make any plans for her summer holiday.

Fortunately, there had been no rain for a couple of days and the fields were dry except behind the potato shed where

Soñadora was parked! Due to the extra weight of Soñadora on the lorry it now required Ron to connect a JCB to assist Glyn in pulling the lorry out of the mud and up the incline to the flat field at the top. This left the ancient Raglan castle to port on the horizon. It was an extraordinary sight. The lorry belonged to our good friend and neighbours Glyn and Shirley Powell.

Glyn driving the Artic Lorry with Soñadora on it

Ron driving the JCB drot getting ready to cross the field to get to the main road

Crossing the field

Raglan Castle on the right

Coming onto the main road

The Police escort checked Soñadora was securely
strapped onto the Lorry before taking to the road

Breathe in only 3 inches to spare

Glyn then continued cautiously across the field while Ron hurried across to the fence. With the aid of the JCB bucket he plucked the wooden council fence out and Glyn drove onto the newly constructed highway. Police on motor bikes had arrived and checked that Soñadora was securely strapped down. We were all very relieved to have got this far safely.

Ron then replaced the fence and returned the heavy duty equipment to another friend, Bernard Thomas. Thank God for good friends. The police escort asked Glyn to keep to a steady speed of 50 mph if possible preventing a build-up of the following traffic.

Everyone following was warned not to try overtaking us. Then we were off! What a trip. The keels were inches off the road going round corners and roundabouts provided a thrill a minute. I had my eyes shut half the time. We were soon in Newport facing our last road obstacle, a low railway bridge. We had to go under it to get into the Container Port. Ron assured Glyn and I that he had measured it. It would be ok, but to me and most people there, it looked impossible. The lorry crept slowly inch by inch. We were through with three inches to spare! We drove into the Container Port parking out of the way of the busy gantry crane. Glyn along with the police escort had achieved a wonderful, safe delivery.

We were told that the cranes for lifting Soñadora were so busy that it would be late evening before they could launch her. So the Police having wished us that all our voyages would be as successful as this one, departed to go about their normal duties.

We had collected quite a party of friends and relatives along the way. It was lunch time so we all adjourned to the nearest pub for a pie and a pint. A well earned break.

After lunch most of our friends departed for their homes feeling well satisfied with the day. Only family, brother Trevor, Pat his wife and Pete, (their son) Terry and Glyn, Ray and his wife Lyn remained. The rain had stopped so we applied the final coat of anti-foul and did all the last minute checks and adjustments. After which we continued partying under the shelter of Soñadora feeling very elated enjoying the food and drink we had brought with us. This would be the first of many parties on the Soñadora.

By 11.30pm the crane was ready to launch   Soñadora. The four big wire hawsers were attached to her chain plates and special strong points. The crane lifted her up off the truck, Glyn backed out and the crane lowered Soñadora to the ground.   It was time to christen her in the traditional manner.

Feeling very happy, near to tears and armed with a bottle of champagne I climbed the ladder and smashed the bottle on her bow saying

"I NAME THIS SHIP *"SOÑADORA"*! GOD BLESS HER AND ALL WHO SAIL IN HER."

There was a loud cheer as the crane raised her into the air just a few minutes to midnight on Sunday April 13th. As the crane moved out over the dock Soñadora must have decided that she didn't want to be launched on the 13th. The crane came to a sudden halt. It had broken down. By the time it had been repaired Soñadora was launched half an hour into the new day of Monday April 14, 1975. She was lowered into the water, the straps were removed and she floated exactly on her water line.

Under the blazing flood lights of the dock she seemed to me to be the most beautiful thing I had ever seen. I turned to Ron. We hugged and kissed congratulating each other. We had made it. I kissed everyone and Ron shook hands all round. It was a wonderful feeling.

In the water at last 14th April 1975 at 9am

Ron, Terry and Ray made Soñadora secure to the dock wall checking to see that everything was safe - no leaking valves, bilge pumps working, etc. Only then did we join in with the others in celebrating the successful launch.

WE HAD MADE IT!

In spite of our late night we were up and on our way early the next day to see if we still had a floating yacht. Yes, she was still floating on her water line looking very pretty with her mast lying along her side deck.

While preparing to move her further along the quayside out of the way of the big ships, we discovered that by sheer good luck she had just missed being launched onto a steel rod, sticking out from the dock side wall on her port side.

Goodness knows what damage it would have done. We were not even at sea yet. I felt quite sick at the thought of it. Someone was definitely looking out for us and would be working overtime by the look of things as we sailed the seven seas.

Soñadora at Newport container port

Chapter 1   The Start of a Dream

The Map on the following page illustrates the route of our first voyage on Soñadora.

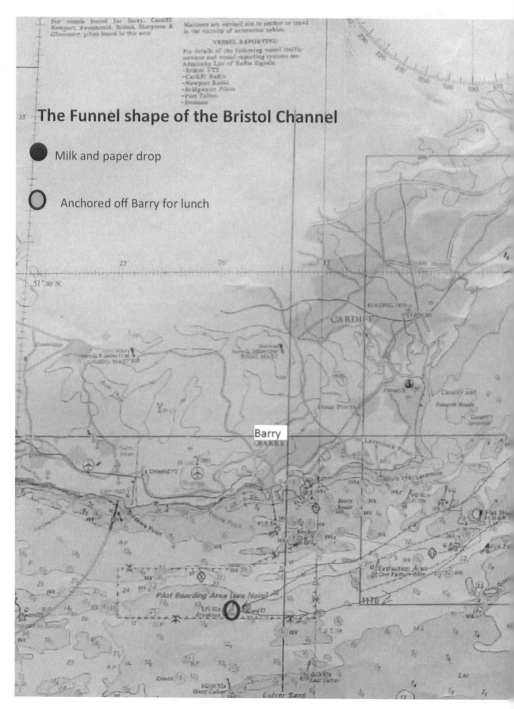

The Funnel shape of the Bristol Channel

● Milk and paper drop

○ Anchored off Barry for lunch

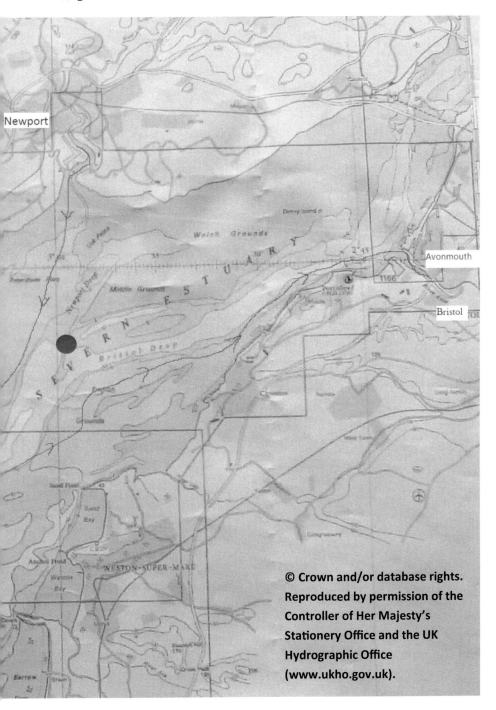

Newport

Avonmouth

Bristol

© Crown and/or database rights.
Reproduced by permission of the
Controller of Her Majesty's
Stationery Office and the UK
Hydrographic Office
(www.ukho.gov.uk).

Chapter 2

All Aboard For Bristol

E recting the mast and rigging was to be carried out by H.R. Spencer of the Isle of Wight while at Bristol City Docks. The Newport docks union at that time were not happy with the presence of private yacht owners, which was a shame, but it was their loss, not ours. So the first trip Soñadora would have to make would be under engine power alone, from Newport to Bristol.

The Bristol Channel, notorious for its fast currents, many sand and mud banks, is no place for the inexperienced. However, fortunately, a work colleague of mine, whose husband, Bob was a Bristol Channel Pilot offered to pilot Soñadora for us. We gratefully accepted his very kind offer of getting her to Bristol safely!

The Bristol Channel has a few unique features, one for having the second highest tidal range in the world (High water to low water, is called the tidal range). The highest high waters takes place in March and September at the Spring and Autumnal equinoxes.

The highest range by only a few centimetres is in the Bay of Fundy, which lies between Nova Scotia and New Brunswick in Canada.

Newport in South Wales UK, however, has the highest tidal range, 15 metres, (50 foot) in the world as there are no cities on the Bay of Fundy.

The higher, High waters are known as Spring tides, (nothing to do with the seasons, probably because they 'spring up' high) and the not so high, High Waters are called Neap tides, (Probably, a Saxon word meaning 'small'). Spring tides occur at Full moon and New moon. The highest tides occur when the rotation of the earth, the gravitational forces of the Sun and Moon, are in alignment.

The Bristol Channel is funnel shaped, and the force of the spring tides 7/8 knots, (8/9) mph creates a wave of water, sometimes as high as 9 feet travelling up the River Severn. This is known as the

" The Severn Bore" and when it happens surfboarders come from miles around to surf on the crest of this wave as it moves up river.

One beautiful sunny Sunday morning with 20 people on board, Ron started the two 60 hp diesel engines and motored out of the Newport Docks into the Bristol Channel with Pilot Bob at the wheel.   Because the tide was ebbing, we had plenty of time, the plan was to motor down to Barry and come back up the Channel to Bristol with the incoming tide.

Getting ready for Bristol, April 14th 1975 at 9 am

As a goodwill gesture Bob had asked Ron if we could deliver the Sunday Newspapers, bread, milk and beer to the English and Welsh grounds light ship which marks the England and Welsh grounds sand bar (see chart), "Of course" said Ron "it is all a new and valuable experience for us."   Bob knew all the crew of the light ship and hailed them as we turned Soñadora around to stem the six knot tidal race, while the crew took our warps (ropes) and made us safe alongside their light ship.

Left to Right Pam, Pat, Carole and Lyn, passengers on Soñadora going to Bristol

Bob Graham Piloting Sonadora to Bristol with Carole, Peter and Wendy

Ron's Mother, Carole, Terry, Bob

Peter, Ray, Bill Bullimore, Lyn, Carole and Ron

After dropping off Milk and Papers to the Lightship

Carole, Peter and Wendy—Summer 1975

We were all invited on board but Ron's dear mother of 79 years remained sitting in the sun, on the foredeck, knitting, and enjoying her first sea trip on Soñadora, loving every minute of it. After a very interesting hour's tour we re-boarded Soñadora and continued on our way to Barry, where we anchored for lunch, while waiting for the tide to turn in our favour.

Sadly, we were told that the manned lightships in the Bristol Channel were being replaced by automatic lights. The crew all said how much they would miss living on the lightships, the end of an era special to life at sea ---- GONE!

We had a very enjoyable trip up the Channel arriving at Avonmouth, just at the right time to continue the six miles up the river Avon, to Bristol, which took us under the M5 motor way bridge. It was fascinating to look up at it but scary.

The Estuary - Avonmouth

Ron relaxing after arriving safely in Bristol enjoying the sun

Brunel's famous Suspension Bridge

We wound our way through the beautiful wooded Avon Gorge admiring Isambard Kingdom Brunel's famous suspension bridge looking much more substantial and attractive than the M5 one. What a brilliant engineer he was! As we arrived at Bristol, the lock gates had just been opened, so we could enter at once.

The Tower Crane stepping Soñadora's mast

We motored through into the city docks tying up just behind another of Brunel's masterpieces, the first steam crane. Because of its shape it is known as the Banana Crane and it still works and can lift 30 ton.

Mike and Joyce Stuart 5225 on their yacht

A little behind us was a large Ferro-cement monohull, belonging to and built by Joyce and Mike Stuart, just outside Newport, on the River Usk, like us they planned to sail it to foreign parts.

Behind them was a large trimaran Tripolka belonging to Charles Pollysky, who had also built it himself. So far it had taken him 6 years and was superbly finished. He was going to sail her back to Poland. It was good to know that we were not the only mad yacht builders. We all soon became good friends.

Charles Pollynsky

Ahead of Tripolka was yet another trimaran. The owner David Blake had kindly taken our warps and helped us to tie up. Ron invited him aboard for a coffee. He noticed our mast on the side deck and asked if we were intending to get her rigged while in Bristol. When informed yes, he offered to arrange to have the mast stepped by a giant tower crane, pointing to one that we could see across the dock working on the Arnolfini building.

He insisted on taking Ron and Terry in his car, over to enquire if that was possible. They returned some time later looking a bit shattered, but with the good news that the crane driver would lift and step the mast holding it in its pod, for rigging. Any time would suit, Ron just had to ask and all for the price of £5. We could hardly believe our good luck thanks to David, who then had to return home with his wife Mona.

Then Ron was able to tell us what a scary time David had given them. David's car turned out to be an open "Triumph Stag" sports car. For him there were only two positions on the accelerator, fully open and closed, even in streams of traffic they had proceeded with tyres screaming, David disregarded their request to walk. While driving back in the same manner, David told Ron that he had just come out of hospital after recovering from his sixth heart attack, which Ron doubted, but it turned out to be quite true. Mona, David's wife, a qualified Nurse later told me his full medical history.

Terry and Ron made a firm vow never under any circumstances to ride with David driving again. We were all amused at their experience. Later on becoming good friends, with David and Mona we told them how he had scared Ron and Terry. We had a good laugh.

While they had been away the rest of us had been packing up ready to go home over the Severn Bridge, to Wales, after a magical first trip. The weather had been perfect and Bob had been the perfect pilot, Soñadora was safe and Mike and Joyce who lived on board their yacht, said they would look out for her, the bus we had booked turned up on time. A truly wonderful day.

We had rented out our house, so the following day Ron returned to live on Soñadora. I had arranged accommodation for

39

myself at the Nurses home at St. Woolos Hospital, Newport, returning to Bristol, Ron, and Soñadora at the weekends.

Another regular visitor from Newport who sometimes stayed the night on Soñadora was Mike Bees who owned a joinery business, and was responsible for most of the excellent carpentry we have on board. I could sometimes get a lift with him jammed in his estate car with the timber.

This was Mike's first experience of yacht carpentry, and he claimed that the few months he had been working on Soñadora had aged him ten years! Like Ron he had found it hard to come to terms with how much longer everything took on a boat with all the curves and nothing level. He was also of a slightly nervous disposition, not improved by an experience he had with some of our elderly relatives while working on board in Newport docks. These docks seemed the ideal place for visitors who could just step on board from the quay or so we thought.

On this occasion Ron's old aunt Flo, arrived with her son Stan, his wife, and Ron's Mother. Stan stepped briskly aboard, holding his Mother firmly by the hand extending his other to shake hands with Ron. Stan's mother, a lady with a heart condition failed to step far enough and disappeared into the small space between the quay and the boat. She dangled on the end of Stan's arm who seemed unaware of her predicament continuing to ask after Ron's health. He looked faintly puzzled when Ron ignoring his offered hand, grabbed Aunty Flo and pulled her up from the depths! She was still, clinging gallantly to a bottle of sherry with her free hand, but was beginning to look a bit blue. We helped her into the saloon and laid her down.

She was quite shocked and had badly grazed her shin which I treated; she spent the rest of her visit lying down sipping the sherry she had had the foresight to bring, and save!

This had upset Mike as he did not like people coming on board while he was working, but worse was to come. Leaving Mike and Ron's Mother on board Ron, and I escorted Aunty Flo, Stan and wife, safely to their car and settled Flo comfortably. Ron's Mother was standing on a cockpit seat waving goodbye. Just as the car moved off we heard an urgent shout from Mike. We dashed back on board to find that Ron's Mother had stepped off the seat falling back into the cockpit, hitting her head on the opposite seat driving her glasses into her eye brow. Blood was spurting everywhere. She insisted she was ok and not to fuss, so she too was laid down in the Saloon, so that I could put a cold compress over her cut eyebrow. She had had a very bad fall resulting in deep bruising, and two lovely black eyes but she was a tough old girl, and I could not keep her lying down for long. After dressing her wound, she also had a glass of sherry, and was soon sitting up wanting to walk about. Consequently, I was cleaning up spots of blood for days later.

This was all too much for Mike so we all sat down and finished off what was left of the sherry. Any conversation with Mike nearly always ended with "is there an end product? Or what is the end product?" When I told him that my sister in-law, Pat, was bringing her elderly relatives, all aged over 75 years the following day, he laughed hysterically. We did not see him again for a week. The thought of what might be the end product of that visit was too much for him to bear.

On Thursday of the second week when we were in Bristol, Ron notified Terry that he had arranged with Spencers and the tower crane driver, to come step and rig the mast on

Soñadora. The crane driver was very skilled; it was a pleasure to watch how easily he positioned the mast in its pod central on the top deck, looking down from his cabin, 100ft above ground. We had already placed a silver coin in the mast pod for the mast to sit on for good luck. The crane driver had to hold the mast in the pod, while the Rigger, also very skilled, supported the mast with temporary rigging, taking all the measurements to enable him to cut the stainless steel rigging to length. The rigging wire required, was too thick for the ends to be swaged on site, so he departed back to the Isle of Wight, to return on the Saturday to complete the job. Terry decided to stay with Ron on Soñadora until the job was finished.

By 4pm on Saturday afternoon the mast was rigged and Soñadora now looked like a real sailing yacht, we had even hanked (hooked) on a sail, and sailed over to the other side of the dock, taking photographs. Her heavy mast was now held up with what looked like masses of 18 ton breaking strain, stainless steel wires, Ron did not intend to have the mast fall down if he could help it.

As we relaxed in the cockpit, it was still a beautifully warm evening, and the men had their shirts off sun bathing, when I suddenly noticed Terry had a row of stitches in his back. I commented on them and he said "Damn, I was supposed to have them out yesterday. Can you take them out for me please Carole?" Thinking he was joking, I said, " well if you don't mind me taking them out with a Stanley knife OK" to my amazement he said "go ahead," so I fitted a new blade to the Stanley knife, sterilized it the best I could, and began to remove them.

As Terry was sitting in the cockpit with his back to the Quay, a group of people passing by on the quayside stopped to watch in amazement, confirming their belief that yacht people were all slightly crazy.

Soñadora's first sail raised
under the watchful eye of
Isambard Brunel's Banana
Crane

The Whitbread race was due to start in the first week of November 1975, it was now August, so time was short. We decided it was time to leave Bristol to carry out our qualifying 1000 sea mile, entrance test.

We rushed around for the last two weeks making preparations, fitting gear, and loading stores. I realised for the first time just how much work was entailed in getting a yacht ready to go to sea out of sight of land. There was no popping down to the corner shop, unless you owned a helicopter! You have to be sure that when you go to sea, however short the trip is, you and your boat are fully prepared for whatever Mother Nature throws at you. But of course, she will always think of something to surprise you, even if you do have a professional crew.

However, eventually, we seemed to be ready, the weather forecast was set fair, so it was arranged for the crew to arrive

Sunday, and departed Bristol on August 18th 1975 for our first real experience of how Soñadora would behave under sail.

It was only convenient for Patrick, Bill, and Terry to come, but as we had to have the same number of crew on board as for the race, numbers were made up by our friends Ray Turner, who had been an officer in the Merchant Navy, but had no experience under sail, and my nephew Peter May who had sailed in his father's catamaran.

The crew were all assembled by Sunday evening, so we all decided, including our Bristol friends to go to the Cabot Cruising club, a converted light ship, afloat in the docks. We had a very enjoyable time, retiring quite early to sleep on Soñadora.

A s the sun rose up from behind the horizon bringing a sense of peace, with a flat calm sea, and clear blue skies, the excitement rose, we would soon know how Soñadora was going to behave under sail. She would be meeting big seas for the first time, her first real test of seaworthiness. We would know if we had a yacht in which we would feel safe in to sail the oceans of the world.

Many sailing ships have left from Bristol, sailing down the Avon Gorge to face the open seas, and the unknown.   It has been a port for more than a thousand years. John Cabot and his son had sailed west from Bristol on the Matthew in the hope of finding a route to Asia and discovered Newfoundland back in 1497.

It was from sugar and slaves that merchants and ship owners had grown rich. Ships had sailed down this river loaded with chains, iron collars, shackles and branding irons, ready for the slaves they were to pick up in Africa, transported and sold to America and the Caribbean Islands as slaves. Ships would return up the Avon River loaded with rum, molasses, sugar and tobacco. Merchants would trade these goods in the Bristol Exchange sealing their bargains by placing their money on the flat topped pillars outside which still exist and from which we get the expression 'trade on the nail'

Bristol was badly bombed during the last war and although the town planners have done their best to finish off what the Germans had begun, there are still many parts of the old Bristol in existence. This includes a few old taverns one of which is the 17th century Llandoger Trow, believed to be the model for the Inn kept by Long John Silver in Treasure Island. It is also supposed to be here that Alexander Selkirk told Daniel Defoe of his adventures on the island of Juan Fernandez, who then turned them into the story Robinson Crusoe.

The floating harbour is still in existence despite plans years ago to fill it in. It was created 1809 by impounding 80 acres at the head of the tidal river Avon using lock gates. This enabled ships to stay afloat in the harbour when the tide went out. It is sometimes visited by our own and foreign navies on courtesy visits.

The old commercial buildings around the dock have mostly been demolished; the shipyard that built many frigates during the war has now been turned into a marina. The S.S. Great Britain, the first steel propeller driven ship built by Brunel, is back in the dry dock where it was built. It has now been fully restored and open to visitors and well worth a visit.

Ron started the engines as our friends cast off our warps from the quay. We motored slowly through the dock, to allow them time to reach the lock before us, ready to take the ropes from us again, as we waited for the lock gates to open. We have the advantage over the old sailing ships as we have engines to take us down the river, where they had to be towed by rowers in long boats.

With very mixed feelings we waved goodbye to our friends as we motored out of the locks into the river behind the trimaran Tripolka on her maiden voyage back to Poland. We went quietly down the river, hoisting the new sails. We were taking our last look at the beautiful gorge passing once again under the Suspension bridge marveling at the genius of Brunel who had managed to span the gorge over one hundred and fifty years ago. Unfortunately, he did not live to see it completed.

Charles Polynsky leaving Bristol bound for Poland. Soñadora following
bound for the Pacific Ocean. 1975

Travelling under Brunel's Suspension Bridge

We passed the village of Pill on our port side, a small inlet, where in the days of the sailing ships the rowers of the long boats lived. It was also where the Channel pilot cutters were based; they used to sail far out into the Atlantic to guide ships back to Bristol. Soon we were passing under the M5 Motorway again. We knew there was plenty of clearance for our mast, but I still watched anxiously as we went underneath.

Once into the Channel the sails were raised, engines stopped, and Soñadora really came to life, as she slipped quietly through the muddy waters of the Severn Estuary. As we left Bristol, Patrick and Terry now started to put her through her paces, tacking and assessing her windward capabilities.

Testing the sails while leaving Bristol

Severn Estuary Avon Docks

The first leg of the race was to windward so the keel area had been increased, Terry seemed happy with her performance. The wind was quite light and soon the tide would turn against us, so we sailed serenely across to Barry where we anchored to wait for it to change in our favour. The first thing one learns about the Bristol Channel, is not to try and win a contest with the tide.

The tide, now being in our favour, we tacked across the channel, the wind strengthening as we went. Just off Ilfracombe there was a loud bang. The mainsail had split along a seam one third from the top. At this time we had no spare main, so we did the only possible thing and anchored in the outer harbour of Ilfracombe to repair the sail. Not a good advertisement for a new sail!

On our way once more, we were travelling very nicely, logging 9-10 knots in every hour. It was very exhilarating. After midnight when the wind was blowing quite strongly, we noticed that the piston hanks, (these attached the number 1 Genoa sail to the fore stay) were coming untied. We changed down to the lighter Genoa No.2 so that repairs could be made to the No.1 not a pleasant job at night with the movement of the boat.

We continued on our way, the seas getting heavier as the winds increased over the tide. A very short steep sea developed, but Soñadora behaved very well, though a few onboard were feeling sea sick We were beginning to understand why it is said that, 'Gentleman never sail to windward!'

At 0300 hours while Bill, Ron and I were on watch, Soñadora began for the first time to start hitting the seas more heavily, shipping water over the foredeck. Bill noticed that once again the piston hanks were coming adrift, this time on the No.2 Genoa. Bill went forward to collect the sail, while Ron released the halyard. As he arrived by the forestay Soñadora shipped a really big sea, which soaked him to the waist He clung on firmly complaining loudly, this was the first time anyone had got really wet.

We got the No.2 sail down and the loose hanks off and as Ron opened the hatch of the sail locker in the forward port bow to stow it, he discovered why we were plunging so heavily. All four sail and anchor warp lockers were full of sea water.

Terry and Ron had decided while in Bristol to raise the floors of these lockers higher above the water line, but had forgotten to refit the self-draining holes and flaps!

Terry calculated that the weight of water in the lockers was equal to having a mini car on the foredeck – no wonder she was putting her nose in. We hove to, (stopped sailing) and pumped out the lockers. Ron drilled temporary drain holes, a difficult job with a hand drill on a heaving boat through inches of fibreglass.

The rest of the trip into the Atlantic, South of Ireland, across

Bill pointing the way to Salcombe for Ron

into the Bay of Biscay and back near Ushant was uneventful.

The weather varied, from 25 knots to flat calm. For a short time we even had thick fog off Ushant which was very frightening experience. One loses all sense of orientation very easily, and in busy waters the mournful sound of the ships foghorns seem to come from all directions. On this occasion as the fog cleared we were treated to a very spooky sight. The top half of a large tanker quietly and suddenly came into view! Appeared to be floating in mid air, the fog obscuring the bottom half, just like in the film Pirates of the Caribbean.

The 1,000 miles had taken several days longer than we had intended, owing to the calms and light winds we had encountered. And once again we were becalmed south off Start Point at 09.00 hours 26th August 1974. The crew, having only limited time, decided that the best plan was to go into Salcombe Kings Bridge Estuary, South Devon where they could get public transport home that day. Soñadora could be sailed to Southampton later for the final   preparations for the race, and leaving England.

We realised how lucky we had been to have had such a trouble free motoring trip from Newport too Bristol because as we tried to motor into Salcombe we discovered that the Ocean outdrives we had fitted were the most dreadful pieces of engineering ever to be visited upon mankind.

Ron eventually managed to get one engine jammed into forward gear with the help of a large bulk of timber and we motored, very carefully through the lovely blue flat calm heaven sent seas into the delightfully sheltered inlet of Salcombe. We anchored off a clean sandy beach in clear water opposite the town. The crew found they had several hours to spare before their trains were due, so we were able to relax and enjoy a beer in the sun on deck, reflecting upon the trip.

Everyone had thoroughly enjoyed it. Terry who had designed Soñadora was more than pleased with her comfort and performance. She had on several occasions achieved 12 miles an hour, and seemed easily and comfortably driven at 8 to 10 knots. Her performance with engines couldn't at this time be assessed although we knew from our Newport to Bristol trip that she could motor comfortably at 7 knots and we had achieved 10 knots for a short time in the calm of Newport docks.

The Oceanic Outdrives was the only disaster. Having seen everyone safely ashore and away to the train, we rowed back to Soñadora happy and contented, to spend our first evening alone since leaving Bristol.

We fed the swans, which had come to visit while we were enjoying a sun downer drink on deck. We then went ashore for a celebration dinner. A delightful change for me, having been ships cook for eight people for ten days!

W e were awakened by a tap tapping on the hulls; Ron went out expecting to find a harbour official demanding his fee. To his delight it was the swans back, demanding breakfast with their beaks! The sun was just rising on another beautiful day. We fed the swans, while taking our own breakfast on deck, watching the holidaymakers slowly emerge onto the beach, a perfect way to start the day.

Ron decided to look at the faulty outdrives, and stripped down the one that had packed up completely. It was obvious that these could not possibly run for long, the design was so terrible. We felt we couldn't rely on the other one running for very much longer and decided to take the broken outdrive for repair. After making enquiries we found Ron could take it to Kings Bridge by bus..

As I sat observing Soñadora across the bay, I realised for the first time how beautiful she looked, and wondered if just the two of us would ever be able to handle her. Ron returned with the ocean outdrive repaired, saying the engineer who did the repair thought it was a piece of farm equipment! On learning it was for a yacht, he laughed saying "it would not last long". With this encouraging news we retired to the nearest pub for lunch. The afternoon was taken up with refitting the repaired outdrive.

The weather and forecast was perfect, so we decided that the two of us would take a chance and sail Soñadora ourselves to Dartmouth the following morning. We could not afford not to make good use of the stable weather. This would be the first time we had actually been at sea on our own, albeit for just 18 nautical miles.

Next morning we were awakened this time by the skipper of a small yacht anchored near to us, who could not raise his anchor, suggesting it might be fouled with ours. Ron explained we were also leaving, and because of the tight anchoring space available when we came in, the crew had laid Soñadora to two anchor's, one fore (front) and one aft (back), this was to stop her swinging round with the tide risking banging into others, Ron suggested to the other skipper that he tied his yacht alongside us, so we could then raise the offending anchors with our electric windlass, untangling them at our leisure, while we would still being held by our second anchor. To this he readily agreed.

Ron started to raise the anchor and sure enough our anchor and his were firmly enmeshed. As they came further out of the water we could see hanging yet a third anchor. It was several seconds before we all realised that it was one of ours, and as the tide was now running out, our two yachts were rapidly heading down river in imminent danger of colliding with the harbour ferry crossing our path just downstream. It was panic stations all round to the great amusement of the onlookers. Ron quickly started the engines, just managing to miss the ferry, to the relief of all concerned. This included the ferry Captain who had made several rude suggestions!! Who could blame him?

I took over manning the wheel while Ron and our obviously experienced yacht neighbour finished sorting things out. It was not the leisurely start we had expected, but at least we were on our way with no harm done. We cast off our friend waving him and his family a cheery good-bye. I suspect we had provided him with an experience he wouldn't forget in a hurry.

We motored out into the open sea on one engine, keeping the other in reserve, having no confidence in the outdrive systems. Thank goodness Ron had had the foresight to get the broken one fixed and re-installed so quickly. It was another lesson learnt; if you can avoid it never leave the maintenance of your yacht for later as you might with a house. Tomorrow may be toooo late!

There was no wind to sail, but it was perfect motoring conditions. We set the autopilot on course, Ron unreeled the fishing lines to trail behind us, while I went below to cook breakfast, after all our excitement we were very hungry. We watched Prawle Point pass close by as we ate our bacon and eggs on deck, looking astern we saw that we had caught our first mackerel.   By the time we were off Start Point we had caught several more.

Crossing Start Bay a small speedboat came alongside and hailed us, we couldn't hear what he was saying so Ron throttled back on the engine; it appeared he was looking for a marker buoy, feeling very knowledgeable, we pointed it out to him.   He waved his thanks and was quickly on his way.

As Ron put the engine back into gear, there was a loud bang and the engine raced. The second outdrive had blown up! We started the other engine and motored on gently towards Dartmouth, two hours later we heaved a sigh of relief as we passed Dartmouth Castle at the mouth of the river.

We motored past the lovely old town of Dartmouth, passing close to Great Britain III a large sleek looking trimaran built especially for Chay Blyth, to take part in the same transatlantic race as us. It looked like it should fly, but we had heard that it had not yet completed its qualifying 1,000 miles. There were construction problems testing out the strength of carbon fibre. In complete contrast there were also some of the old Tall Ships used in the Onedin Line an old TV series filmed in the area.

We motored on up the river and dropped anchor in the quiet waters between wooded hills, and cooked the fresh mackerel for lunch, they were delicious! After a short rest, absorbing the peace of the surroundings we returned down river anchoring opposite the town.

It was the week of Dartmouth Naval Regatta so we had a grandstand view of the rowing competitions. It was very exhausting to watch! We were forced to have several beers just to sustain us, as we looked on.

That evening we went ashore to explore the town, and telephoned Terry to let him know where we were. He was pleasantly surprised, and arranged to come down late Friday evening to help us sail Soñadora to Southampton over the weekend. We were glad of his intended company.

We had a meal, and relaxed afterwards in the bar of an interesting old Inn, where one could imagine smugglers bringing in casks of Brandy to be drunk in front of the huge open fire place... We talked over the events of the day, and decided that we had not totally disgraced ourselves on our first solo trip. It began to look more and more that the years of planning, and hard work had been worthwhile.

On Friday we had a quiet relaxed day not having many preparations to make for the trip to Southampton. We went ashore that evening to collect Terry who had brought his wife Pam and son Graham. Returning, to the quay we found that a naval launch had backed into our dinghy knocking off our out-board motor, which was fortunately attached to a safety cord hanging 2ft under water. They apologised, offering to tow us back over to the yacht, an offer we were glad to accept, because a 7ft rubber dinghy is not the best of things to row when heavily loaded. In order to tow us at a suitable speed so we did not get wet, they were forced to just tick their engines over.

However, after a little while we were glad to cast off and row as the exhaust fumes from their outboard were just about killing us! It was midnight when we got back onboard. We listened to the shipping forecast, which was favourable for us with winds up to 20 knots. Terry, suggested we take advantage of the fair winds and have a night sail. The winds had been very light and variable and Ron doubted our capabilities to motor, the wind was too good to miss. Having prepared Soñadora we lifted the anchor, I took the wheel and motored her to the mouth of the river, while Ron and Terry hanked on and raised the sails.

As we entered the open sea, Ron stopped the engines and we started to sail very briskly close to the wind. When we had cleared Berry Head the wind came more abeam and strengthened to 25 knots and we really started to fly. It was pitch black scary, but very exhilarating, increased by the brilliant phosphorescence of the twin wakes leaving long blazing trails behind us as we touched 18 knots. The winds now varied between 20 - 25 knots with brief gusts to 30.

Berry Head light house was shining brightly; it is the highest and shortest in England, highest because no other light stands on so high a headland, the shortest because the lens is only 6 foot above the ground.

We had soon left the lights of Torquay behind and passed the other seaside towns in quick succession. By this time there was quite a sea running and we were smashing through the flying spray, coloured red and green by our navigation lights.

Soñadora seemed to be loving it, and so were Ron, Terry, and I, but unfortunately Pam and Graham were not feeling their best and they were trying to sleep in the saloon. I should not have made curry for dinner! I was learning the do's and don'ts of going to sea.

We were keeping a careful eye out for shipping, and, other small craft, making sure Soñadora was not over pressed. There seemed no need to reef down, so we thundered on through the night. We gave Portland Bill a good offing and headed for the Isle of Wight and the Needles channel.

We entered Southampton waters, and headed up the river making for Wilmot's shipyard, where we were to berth Soñadora by the Solaris slipway. We had had an exhilarating sail, averaging nearly 15 knots the fastest passage so far, eventually we had to drop the sails and start the engine. Motoring up past the floating bridge maneuvering with difficulty having only the one engine, we berthed as arranged without mishap.

We made Soñadora secure and safe and went with Pam and Terry back to their home in the New Forest, where we had hot baths, and a good meal. Relaxing afterwards, we enjoyed once again talking over the trip, adding a few more items to the list of things to be done, before leaving England. The most important of them being the boom which we had noticed was too weak, and of course we had to do something about our outdrives. There was no doubt that the next two months were going to be very hectic!!

O n Sunday morning we returned to Southampton and Soñadora to discover that the old motor torpedo type craft that we had moored Soñadora alongside had gone aground when the tide went out and was now leaning heavily upon her, while on the other side there was another large barge making her the meat in a sandwich. There was obviously a lot of weight being put upon Soñadora because the lorry tyres we had used as fenders were flattened, though it didn't seem to be doing her any damage. As soon as the tide came in we moved her to a safer berth nearby.

At this time I had not yet given up my post as a Nursing Officer, so had to return to Newport ready for work on Monday I was glad I only had one month more before leaving, as it was going to be hard to settle down and concentrate on work after the exciting time we had just spent on Soñadora. Ron was going to stay on her, continuing the work while I stayed in Newport at the Nurses Home.

The next few weeks passed quickly. Ron had bought an old Austin 1100 for £45 and came down to visit on the weekends, which we spent with Pat and Trevor. It was good for Ron to have a complete break away from boats for a while.

Returning to the Nurses Home late one Sunday night, brought back memories of the last time we had done this, just before we were married. We had crept along the corridors trying not to laugh, to my bedroom, Ron with a large feather mattress on his back that had been given to us as a present. This was under the incredulous gaze of two young nurses and their boyfriends, who were trying to keep out of my sight as a senior nurse, for they too were breaking the rule that said "No boyfriends allowed in at night". Ron must have looked very funny as he wrestled the ungainly mass into my room.

The month flashed by. At last I had finished work and after a farewell party with many good wishes and very mixed feelings. I loved my nursing career.

I returned to Southampton where chaos reigned, but progress had been made. It had been decided to try Soñadora out in a local multihull yacht race from the Isle of Wight to the Shambles Lighthouse Buoy, to check out new sails, boom, and other gear that had been fitted.

Modifications had been made to the outdrives by a local engineering firm. They had done all that was possible to improve them, but nobody was hopeful that they would last very long. Most of the intended crew for the Whitbread Race were able to come, but unfortunately, Bill had to withdraw because of a serious family illness, a shame for both him and family. The evening prior to the race, we motored over to Cowes ready for the early start.

In the morning the wind was very light and from the start we all more or less drifted with the tide down towards Portland Bill, rounding the light buoy. After midnight there was practically no wind, by early dawn we had only covered a few miles of the return leg so we decided to abandon the race and motor back to Southampton. This had not given us much chance to evaluate any of our new equipment other than the VHF Radio which worked very well. However, the weather was beautiful and it was good to be on the water again after a month in dock. As we entered Southampton waters the port outdrive once again broke up. It had run for exactly 10 hours!! We continued on the starboard engine, this time returning to beach her in front of a large shed on a muddy beach.

We sat in the cockpit having a few drinks while the tide slowly went out, making more lists of things to do. By this time we had lists of lists, and Ron who could not stand being organised at the best of time and hated lists, was getting more fed up by the minute, and clutching his drink he walked up to the bow to get away from it all.

The tide had receded and the bows were high in the air, as he leant over the pulpit to look down from the boat it gave a little lurch, tilting forward like a see-saw. Ron rushed back to the cockpit, shouting, as she settled back down again with a thump!! "Don't anyone move I will go down to see what has happened."

He hooked a ladder onto the stern and gingerly lowered himself down into the thick mud which covered his feet. He wallowed down along the side of the boat and from what we could gather from the little bits of information that interspersed the curses. Soñadora had come to rest on her keels over a large baulk of timber right on the point of balance. Without our combined weight at the stern she would have tipped forward onto her bows causing serious damage.

We had to stay where we were while Ron hunted around for long blocks of timber to put under the point of her bows reaching to the ground. It was not an easy task with no one else around to help as we dared not move. By this time he was covered in thick black horrible mud and not very happy. Our enforced idleness had not been too difficult, we just felt guilty at not being able to assist him, though I am sure our cheery shouts of encouragement had helped! Not as much however, as the hot shower, clean clothes, and a very large Gin and Tonic did.

Although this turned out to be a light hearted incident it was one of our first lessons in safety, awakening our minds to the thousand and one snares and pitfalls. As our voyage around the world continued we were to find out from our own experiences and those of others, that it isn't the big storms, huge seas, and the obvious that kill you. Often as not it is the little things, some so simple and avoidable, some so bizarre that only good luck can save you. In this case even though we had examined the place where we had intended to beach her, the timber had not been visible, the tide had not gone out enough to show the timber and it had looked the best position for Soñadora. It was sheer good luck that we had sufficient people on board, sitting in the right place, when Ron had walked up to the bow deck. That night as soon as we floated, we pulled Soñadora further up the beach, taking lines ashore and making fast to the shed behind us.

Ron and Carole testing Terry's Oyster Catcher dinghy boarding Soñadora in Southampton waters

Ron had discovered a little cafe down by the floating bridge, which served baked potatoes with various fillings. They were delicious and this little café was to provide us with many a quick meal in the busy days ahead.

We were interested to see in another shed close by, a large plywood catamaran being built, this was also entered in the Whitbread Race. It was obvious, even to us that there was no way that this could be ready on time to take part. We knew that Great Britain III was still having difficulties and there was much doubt as to whether she would qualify in time. We were becoming a little concerned as to who our competitors might be. As far as we knew we were the only yacht that had as yet qualified. The organisers kept telling us of various other boats that had entered; saying there was no shortage of competitors.

We were not too surprised however when the secretary of the organising committee, contacted us, asking if we would mind the Race being delayed for 2 weeks to enable Great Britain III to qualify. We were glad to agree as it would give us more time for preparations as well.

Soñadora floated with every tide, so Terry lent us a little dinghy which had an endless rope with which we pulled ourselves the fifteen yards to and from the shore. The dinghy was a prototype of one of Terry's discarded brain storms, which he had aptly named The Oyster Catcher. In theory this was an interesting idea, it had two pod-like hulls joined together by hinges, forming a small catamaran when open and a secure lockable container for oars, etc when closed and was easy to tow when shut. However, we discovered it had the unnerving tendency, when in use to close and entomb anyone in it as it sank to the bottom!

Ron using the endless rope to get the Oyster Catcher
to Soñadora

63

One particular morning I had been ashore shopping, and on returning called for Ron to assist me aboard. I placed my shopping in the dinghy and sat on the stern where I felt safe from entrapment, however, Ron asked me to sit further forward. This I felt disinclined to do, so an argument ensued. Whereupon Ron pulled hard on the rope, the dinghy left the shore with a quick jerk throwing me backwards into the water the unexpected cold shock on entering the water brought my side of the argument to an abrupt halt. A man in a wooden dinghy close by observed all of this with astonishment. I climbed back into the dinghy, and this time Ron managed to get me aboard. After a shower and change of clothes I was still not speaking to Ron.

At this time we had the refrigeration engineers aboard installing our refrigeration and deep-freeze systems, one of the men had to go into town for some freezer unit parts, I decided that I had had enough of boats and husbands for one day, so asked for a lift with him back into town.

I lowered myself carefully into the dinghy clasping on to the ladder to   hold it steady for the engineer to get in. He got half way down the ladder, placed one foot on the edge of the dinghy pressing it down level with the water which then started to fill the dinghy. He froze and would not move up or down the ladder or take his foot off the dinghy. The dinghy not liking this sudden assault (definitely female) decided to fold up and started to sink.

I just had time to hand my handbag to the chap to put it up on deck who was still hanging on grimly to the ladder with both legs in the water. I once again found myself immersed, this time swimming for my life, while the chap continued to complain bitterly. He didn't see the funny side of it at all. Ron just turned away in disgust telling the man to get back on board.

The wooden dinghy man was still close by, I think by now

he thought that Ron was trying to drown me! He rowed over and said "Let me take you ashore missus, you'll be safer with me." He got me aboard his dinghy, but I asked him to take me to Soñadora. By now both Ron and I had seen the funny side of it all and were laughing, so once again I came aboard for another shower and a change of clothes.

Ron gave the refrigeration chap (who was still not amused), a clean towel and a dry pair of trousers after which he demanded to go ashore, alone this time, taking the view it was all somehow my fault! As I was now talking to Ron, I did not want to go ashore anyway.

It was, only a few days after agreeing to the delayed start of the race, that Ron was astounded to be asked by a workman in the yard "What are you going to do now, that the race is cancelled?" Ron said "What do you mean I haven't heard anything about it?" The chap said, "It's true enough, everyone in the yard knows." Ron straight away telephoned the race organiser and sure enough it was correct.

We were rather upset at the off hand manner in which the whole affair was handled, with no apologies for the considerable trouble we had gone to for the race. It was sometime later that we received a short note enclosing the refund of our entrance fee and I suppose as some sort of peace offering, four cases of canned beer arrived. The most expensive beer ever!!

Mr. Jack Hayward who had sponsored the £200,000 Great Britain III yacht, was also justifiably annoyed. Mr Hayward had done much to enhance the prestige of British yachting, sponsoring Great Britain III etc. He was instrumental in the return of Brunel's original Great Britain from the Falkland Islands to Bristol where she is being restored. He was quoted as saying, "I feel very strongly that a firm of the calibre of Whitbread's, having agreed to sponsor a race of this kind would then pull out 2 weeks before the start. It has shaken the whole yachting world."

However, there was nothing we could have done about it; the entry form had given Whitbread's the right to make all decisions. While we could appreciate Whitbread's concern for safety, by not allowing unqualified yachts to start, we had been led to believe right to the end that there were other foreign yachts entered including one Solaris with an all girl crew. We were to learn later when reaching Gibraltar, and meeting the owner that he had turned down the suggestion of entering the race at the outset. We have never really forgiven Whitbread's, but still drink their beer!!

Terry contacted all the crew and by this time all their booked holidays, and air flights back from Florida were cancelled. Most were still keen to cruise across the Atlantic, and at Patrick's suggestion we decided to make our destination Antigua.

Ron had looked upon the cancellation of the race as a very lucky reprieve. He had been getting less and less happy about leaving England with the boat and himself so untried and with only one outdrive operational, and the other very doubtful. He had visions of ending up in some foreign part with no facilities to put things right. He thought it more prudent to spend another year around the coast of Britain, to get everything tried, tested and working. We would become more competent to handle the boat, and of course he was right in theory. But on the other hand I was certain we should go, we had seen so many people who had had the same dream as us, put off starting. Time after time for all sorts of reasons many people with these dreams never made it. The need for security is so deeply embedded in them, that they are too afraid to let go, never realising that there is no such thing as security. As a nurse I know that death is only three short minutes away at anytime. Anyway I just hate quitting! I didn't think this would apply to us, but I didn't want to give it the chance.

We met Terry in the lounge bar of the Yacht Pub just outside the yard, and discussed the cancellation of the race, and what to do next. Terry and I were keen to go anyway, but Ron was adamant that we should stay.

Terry pointed out the advantages of going, Patrick would still teach Ron navigation, we would have thousands of sea miles of ocean sailing experience, and he was quite confident that Soñadora was very seaworthy. I pointed out that we already had stores on board for 7 crew for a month, and stores for us for 12 months, including a 10 cubic foot deep freeze full of meat.

It was no good; Ron was not going to be persuaded! I felt so down and to crown it all, the pub's radio started to play Roger Whitaker's recent hit 'There's a ship lies rigged and waiting in the harbour.' I just burst into tears, not something I do every day. Poor Ron, he had enough on his plate without me cracking up. He slapped his hand on the table, saying, "That's it I can't stand it anymore, we will go, anything to get away from this bloody lot!" and so the major decision was taken and I still think it was the right one. When we returned to Bristol Docks five years after cruising the world, the two couples who had planned similar trips were still there. Though there had been times when we regretted leaving before Soñadora was completely finished, the important thing was WE DID GET AWAY.

To meet Patrick's business commitments in Antigua it was essential that we left not later than the 8th November 1975. Allan and Bill had decided for family reasons not to come, and were replaced by Donald and Brian. We now had a full crew again.

Patrick had arranged with the service agents of our life raft, that in return for using Soñadora in a demonstration in the use of a life raft to be filmed for TV, they would service our life raft free of charge.

By this time she had been anti-fouled and the next day, Patrick and Terry came down for the life raft demonstration. For this we had to be afloat so it was urgent that we moved off the mud at the very height of the tide. Ron was busy working in the engine room, and kept shouting up to Patrick who was sorting out the charts, "Is it high water yet?" "No," back came the answer from Patrick. However, when Ron eventually emerged, we had by some strange chance missed it! There wasn't enough water to move her. Patrick said "not to worry Ron, it is a peculiarity of the Southampton area that they have two high waters, one a couple of hours after the other, we will catch the second one," but there was not enough water on the second high tide either. Ron was not amused. Fortunately, a power boat that Terry had designed called the Corvette had just been launched, so he arranged with Bill the owner and friend to use his boat for the life raft demonstration.

The camera man, his assistant plus three men arrived and sat up on the fly bridge of the Corvette, not a smile on their faces, looking down on us; the three men were all dressed the same, black suits, trilbies, and umbrellas. They reminded us of three crows!

The weather was fine, and sunny, with no wind. The service agents had brought three life rafts in case as they put it, "The first one didn't open," this didn't instill much confidence in us about our life raft! Happily the first one inflated. Several of us had dressed for the part in foul weather gear and one by one leapt gallantly on to the life raft's canopy, rolling in through the opening. It could be quite painful for those already inside, if they did not get out of the way quickly.

Apart from one man putting his foot through the canopy all went well. By now we were all laughing, with the exception of Ron, who was still mad about the fiasco of not getting off the mud, and refused to have anything to do with what he called "this incredible cock-up." Though it did eventually bring a smile to 'the three crows' faces and even to Ron's. The whole scene was so unrealistic, the flat calm sea, nothing like the rough seas that normally prevail, when poor yachtsmen have to take to their life rafts, with huge waves, and a floundering yacht, wet, cold and frightened silly.

The following day Ron got Soñadora off the mud, and tied up to a quay just opposite. This had become vacant when the latest 'Solaris' had been collected by its proud and lucky owner. It was quite a dilapidated quay, with several nasty iron girders sticking out under the waterline. Anchors were laid out with lines to bow and stern to hold the yachts off the quay wall. The rise and fall of the tide made it necessary to climb up and down a metal ladder making it difficult for loading.

There were only a few days left before we sailed, and the compass adjuster had yet to come and swing the compass. This had been arranged for the afternoon and when he arrived at 2pm we started the engine and cast off. With only one engine it was a difficult place to get out from, requiring much use of forward and reverse gears and this proved just too much for our remaining outdrive which promptly gave up the ghost. Fortunately, we were still within rope throwing distance of the quay, and with the assistance of a kind onlooker we were made fast back to the quay. The compass adjuster left in a huff, the compass still UNSWUNG.

By now Ron was completely fed up, and seemed to lose interest. I couldn't blame him, he had worked so hard and everything seemed to be falling apart under his nose.

To reduce weight because of the race much of the interior fittings of the boat had not been installed. It had been planned to have them shipped to Florida for fitting there, this plan having been cancelled, there were men now all over the boat fitting as much as possible, and loading aboard the rest. It was sheer chaos! But now, being without engines was what upset Ron the most, though Patrick and the crew seemed not at all concerned, saying that Soñadora was primarily a sailing yacht. They were confident that they could sail her anywhere, and indeed many yachts had sailed right around the world without engines. Ron had given up caring anyway, but they managed to allay the few doubts I was beginning to have.

It was decided to ignore the outdrives altogether, so Terry arranged that when we left on the following Saturday the Corvette, would tow us out into the Southampton waters. We would take the compass adjuster with us to swing the compass, and he would return on the Corvette.

The last few days were one mad rush; the only thing that cheered Ron up for a little while was selling our little 1100 Austin to another yachtsman for £45, the first time in his life he said he had not made a loss on a car. The owner of another catamaran Snuggle Puss, impressed by my endless activity presented me with a large soft toy parrot labelled 'Action Bird', much to everyone's amusement. It remained a beloved member of our crew, amusing many children.

On Friday night Terry's wife Pam gave a farewell party. There were so many of us, with the crews' family and friends. Pam had worked hard; it was a huge success and just what we needed. It also gave us a chance to thank everyone for their help and support over the last five years.

Quite a few of us slept on board Soñadora that night. Early in the morning Bob the foreman from Solaris delivered some diesel fuel in 44 gallon drums and siphoned it into our tanks and there were still men working on board, putting things down every hatch, into any space they could find.

Ron and I decided to leave them to it, while we went to get our international driving licenses. It was a relief to get away on our own for a couple of hours. When we returned, we found that

Mona and David had flashed down from Bristol. David looked like he was just about to have heart attack No.7, I quickly sat him down and gave him a triple brandy; he had been told that doubles were bad for him!

Pat and Ron's mother were busy feeding the multitude. Then the Customs Officials, arrived to seal the duty-free goods that had just been delivered on board. It was real duty-free then at 10 shillings a bottle for spirits. I hope I am managing to give you some idea of the absolute pandemonium of it all. It would have to be the most terrible way to depart on a cruise, in the future we always slipped quietly out of port with the minimum of farewells, and never until we were completely ready as could be.

Bill, his wife and Terry arrived with the Corvette and tied astern at 14.00 hours. They organised some farewell drinks on board, and very kindly presented us with a set of whisky glasses to wish us Bon Voyage. By 15.00 hours we were ready, the big moment had come.

This seemed a good time for Ron and I to thank everyone again who had assisted us, particularly the men from 'Solaris' who, had worked so well under such difficult circumstances. Terry and his father, who had wallowed in the mud helping Ron to anti-foul, and his mother for her support. Pam his wife helped me with our catering, and our families and friends, whose comfort and support made such a difference to us, and all the other people too numerous to mention who helped in all sorts of ways. Also to Colin Swale who cycled up at the last moment with a bottle of wine and a little china pussy cat, wishing us well. I put the Cat with the Parrot. I have them still and more.

"All ashore who are going ashore", Ron shouted, as he heaved the ladder onto the quay. Soñadora was laying port side to the quay with her stern to the sea. Terry was on the Corvette helping Bill slowly bring her astern of Soñadora to get a towline onto her starboard bow.

Everyone looked on with astonishment, as Ron suddenly started to leap up and down waving his arms, shouting wildly. The word quickly went round that Ron had cracked at last! In fact he had suddenly remembered the two lines running out to the anchor that held us off the projecting steel of the quay. It was too late, by the time Terry had realised the danger and reacted, the stern line was now firmly around one of the propellers of the Corvette.

Everything came to a halt, engines were put out of gear the propeller was turned anti-clock wise, but we could not get the line off. Ron in old clothes was just about to leap into the water to free the line, when Bill dressed in a beautifully tailored suit appeared with a knife, shot down his boarding ladder at the stern, into and under the water and freed the line from around his prop and quite unconcerned about the whole incident, handed both lines to Ron. He stepped back onto his Corvette to much cheering from the crowd on the quay. He really proved to be a great guy!

We handed the other anchor line up to the wharf men on the quay. The tow line was attached to our bow, and all other lines were stowed, we didn't want a repeat performance. The Corvette slowly towed Soñadora out into the Southampton waters so the Compass adjuster could do his job before it was too dark for him to see the land marks for his bearings.

Fortunately, there were no gross errors in our main compass, which is of the remote type, positioned well away from any magnetic influences, so the adjuster was able to correct it very quickly, with the Corvette maneuvering Soñadora as he directed. The Corvette then came alongside Terry came aboard, and the compass adjuster boarded the Corvette. The crew, Ron and I were all on deck waving goodbye to everyone, tears were flowing. I hate goodbyes. The down side of cruising is that you get so many of them. By now the tears of farewell had turned to tears of laughter, I was thinking that if we can get into this sort of mess with all these people helping us, what fun we will have on our own.

Minutes later we were on our way, Pat, Trevor and the crew's wives were all on the Corvette busy taking photographs of us, which due to poor light never came out. The wind was starting to get up; Force 5 to 6 was forecast, so we were not going to be short of wind.

We were now under sail and on our way, our departure had been so uproarious, that it was only now it had all become a reality. My feelings were very mixed, I was thoroughly tired, but so excited and relieved that we had actually started, but sad at saying goodbye to everyone and to Britain. I sought out Ron, and we had a long quiet hug, he said "Well, come hell or high water we are on our way, at least it should be sunny in Antigua." It had not been the departure we had planned in our dreams, and I could tell Ron was convinced we had done the wrong thing, but I knew nothing would make him go back now.

As we were passing Lymington we sighted navigation lights quickly closing in on us. To our surprise it was the Corvette. They had dropped off the compass adjuster and were heading back to their berth in the marina at Lymington, and our families were still on board. We all went out onto the aft deck, Ron coming up from the engine room, where he had started an engine to charge the batteries.

Yet again we all waved and shouted goodbye. As the two boats drew apart I turned to go into the saloon to have a little cry in private. Seeing them again had been the last straw, I was getting very emotional. My eyes being filled with tears I was not looking where I was walking and I stepped over the side and hurtled straight down backwards into the engine room. Ron had left the engine room hatch open!! Fortunately, I had hooked my right leg and one arm over the combing of the hatch opening. This saved me from crashing down on my back onto the engine. As if my predicament wasn't serious enough, the heavy hatch cover chose that moment to close onto my head. I must have cried out, for the next thing I knew Ron and Terry had an arm and leg apiece and had heaved me out, carrying me into the saloon.

I was in considerable pain, but had a mental picture of how ridiculous the whole episode must have looked. I was now laughing and crying at the same time. Poor Ron and Terry looked on in confusion, not knowing what action to take first, but relieved that there was obviously nothing too wrong physically, mentally was another matter!

Having recovered a little I checked myself over and was relieved to find that my left arm was only bruised, but my right knee was badly strained. I rested quietly on my bunk; consuming a large scotch that Ron had the presence of mind to bring me.

Patrick had organised the crew into watches and whilst everyone was getting themselves sorted out, the winds were increasing, allowing Soñadora to sail well. I had recovered enough to cook the evening meal of lamb chops and mashed potatoes; at this stage everyone had a good appetite, so it was much appreciated. Because I was doing the cooking I was not standing any watches, so I took a sleeping tablet and two painkillers and retired to my bunk for a good night's sleep.

The wind continued to increase to gale force and by midnight we were running down channel under storm jib only. It was a very rough start to our trip, which was unfortunate, because the crew hadn't had time to adjust to the motion. With the exception of Ron who had, thank goodness never been sea sick, we were all under the weather to some extent or another, and certainly not interested in breakfast.

The galley was in a terrible state but none of the crew were in a fit state to tackle the job of cleaning it up. Ron insisted that I stayed in bed until he had done it, a two hour job. By now I too was very sea sick and it was useless to take anti-seasick tablets when continually vomiting. I knew that if I didn't recover soon I would have to give myself an intramuscular injection of stemetil. I lay there for two hours dreading the thought of this, I hate having injections though I have given thousands, but always to others not to myself.

By lunchtime although the weather had improved, I still felt terrible, so plucking up courage I gave myself the injection into my damaged leg, on the principle, that I might as well have all the pain in one area. Stemetil really is a marvellous anti sea sickness drug and within the hour I was up and offering to inject the crew, who took one look at the syringe and declined with the exception of Terry. He had a macabre interest in all things medical and he was never happier than when deeply engrossed in my medical books. I don't know if it was the improving weather, or the threat of a large injection, but by late, afternoon the crew had all pretty well recovered, although some still had to take the sea sick tablets.

We had made fairly good progress down channel all day with no alarms or excitements and as it went dark Patrick introduced us to the custom of Happy Hour a novelty to us, but apparently the custom on racing yachts, where during the day alcohol is not allowed and so they set aside one hour in the evening to socialise and reflect on the days happenings with a drink. This put Ron off racing more than ever, being of the opinion that all his hours should be happy! The events of the trip so far where discussed, and seemed to be satisfactory and we were looking forward to better weather as we progressed further south. It was agreed that once we had cleared the Scilly Isles we should get a good way west (westing) in order to avoid being swept into the

Bay of Biscay.

After Happy Hour we were all able to enjoy a good cooked dinner. My leg was still very painful and I was unable to bend it; I had obviously seriously damaged the ligaments of my knee. The crew insisted that I should rest it as much as possible, so leaving them to do the washing up, I retired to bed.

Later that night the wind increased to gale force, and once again we had a very rough night, but we were still making progress in the right direction. The next morning the sun came out, the wind died away, and we even managed to have lunch sitting on the foredeck, watching some dolphins playing around the hulls.

As we sat eating our cheese and biscuits and drinking tea, we thought perhaps we had it made, from here on, it was going to be bikinis and sun oil, but alas it was not to be. By the time evening came, the winds were once again gale force, we were reefed right down, and I am afraid the crew didn't enjoy their Happy Hour and had little appetite for dinner. In fact I would not have bothered cooking at all if it wasn't for Ron who could always eat and felt deprived if he didn't get his victuals.

The weather became so bad that by midnight we dropped all sails, and laid a hull for the first time, the winds were gusting to 60 knots, and we had no idea how Soñadora was going to react to these conditions. As the night wore on it became clear that this was the correct strategy, Soñadora rode the huge seas like a seagull with just an occasional thump as the odd rogue wave hit us. We were all very relieved in fact we had quite a restful night.

In the morning the winds had reduced to force 7 southwesterly so we were sailing again, it was now that a decision was made which was to completely change the results of the voyage for everyone. The wind had gone even more southerly, so the choice of laying a course further southwest out into the Atlantic or southeast towards the coast of Portugal, had to be made. Patrick as skipper, after discussing the course options with everyone, made the decision that the south-easterly course towards Portugal would be the most favourable.   Ron queried the chance of us getting embayed, in the much feared Bay of Biscay, which is notorious for being the home to some of the Atlantic Oceans fiercest weather. Patrick assured Ron, that there was no chance!!

We had a brisk sail through the day, but sure enough during our Happy Hour, David who was on the wheel, shouted through the cabin door that he thought it would be a good idea to put a reef in the main and change down to a smaller headsail as the wind was beginning to get up again. We sat clutching our drinks in the warmth thinking about this, trying to make a decision which sail to change down to, when David stuck his head in again shouting, "Whatever you are going to do - do it quickly or you will lose the bloody mast, I'm showing over 35 knots on the wind indicator."

He and Donald who were on watch had already eased the sheets and the rest of the crew rushed out to help change the sails, but by the time they had the headsail down the wind had gone up to 40-45 knots. They dropped and stowed both sails. And once again we were laying a hull with the wind increasing all the time.

For the next three days the wind never dropped below 45-50 knots, and on one occasion the needle was right around the dial on our wind speed instrument. This meant force 11, (60 knots) for minutes at a time and eventually in one severe gust, the strut on the top of the mast which carried the revolving wind cups blew right off!!

We were quite comfortable laying a hull, so while listening to the radio, we were very sad to hear that some fishing boats had foundered and fifteen lives had been lost. The seas were really mountainous and because of the spray, visibility was practically nil. We kept a look out, but it was not very effective and we hoped our radar reflector was efficient, and that any ship near us would be keeping a good radar watch.

The winds were so strong that it was difficult to stand up outside and because of my leg, I had not been allowed to go out. One night when Ron was on watch he took me out into the cockpit, holding me firmly, the wind was blowing so strongly it was difficult to breathe as I faced it, but the moon was shining brightly and I could see the huge waves as they marched towards us in rows with the spray blowing off their crests. It seemed they must crash down upon us, but at the last moment, Soñadora would rise up like a seabird, and the waves would pass harmlessly underneath us. Every few minutes you would hear a hiss and a roar, this was a wave riding over the tops of the other waves, which would hit us as it went through, covering us with spray. It was a magnificent and terrifying sight, but I felt so safe and secure on Soñadora with Ron, that I didn't at that time feel at all afraid, but anxious and worried for the safety of the crew, for if they found they couldn't sail Soñadora away from the coast we would be lucky to get ashore alive. The waves would pound us to pieces, and we felt we were all too young to die just yet.

As the days passed, we were driven steadily back into the Bay of Biscay. There seemed to be no prospect of the wind turning in our favour and we were becoming concerned that if we continued on our present course, we would be driven onto the coast. Because we had had no intention of coming anywhere near this part of the ocean, we had no charts of the area. The only information we had was the Bay of Biscay Pilots List of Lights and our Radio Direction Signals. Patrick had been using our Radio Direction Finders signals to fix our position for the last few days and had a fair idea of where we were. A decision was made to try and reach the coast of Spain, taking into account our position and the information available in the 'Pilot' book it seemed that Gijon a port on the north coast of Spain was the most favourable if we could carry a sail.

We were all pleased to be doing something positive at last, boredom had began to set in. Apart from reading, sleeping, and eating the main occupation since the loss of our wind speed indicator had been looking at the state of the sea and comparing it to the illustrations in Reeds Almanac and arguing one with another according to the optimism or pessimism of the individual as to how strong the wind was and trying to guess the height of the waves. None of which was easy from a small craft.

Terry and Brian, the only smokers of the group were beginning to feel like lepers. Because of the no smoking below decks rule, they were forced to cower in the bottom of the cockpit whenever they wanted to smoke. Just putting their heads through into the saloon door to light up would bring down the wrath of us all upon them and as likely as not, having managed to light up before they could obtain a satisfying lung full of smoke, a dollop of sea would extinguish the cigarettes. We would hear their loud curses and plaintive cries of distress!!

When they came to put up the storm jib which was the only sail small enough to carry in these conditions, it started to tear along a seam. It must have been weakened the last time it was used. Donald had to turn to and repair it, not the easiest of tasks as it was made of very thick sailcloth.

By 10am we were under way at last making slow progress towards the coast and we hoped to be in the safety of Gijon harbour before dark. As the coast came into view there was no sign of Gijon and as there was only one direction in which we could sail, east along the coast, hoping that we were to the west of Gijon. The RDF (radio direction finder) while a good aid in these conditions was not very accurate. The motion of a small boat makes the reading of compass bearings very difficult, especially without a chart of the area. Patrick had made up a rough one on graph paper, giving the longitudes and latitudes of the RDF stations obtained from our list of Radio Stations. It was no real surprise that we found ourselves east of Gijon and sailing away from, rather than towards it.

By this time we were barely two miles off the coast and we

could see the waves crashing up the low cliffs, like a waterfall in reverse. It was now that the crew had to be sure of sailing Soñadora anywhere without engines as using the storm jib we were clawing off the coast as best we could, but we did not know exactly where we were.

Ron wasn't very confident that if a headland came into sight that we would be able clear it. He asked me to put all our papers and other important things into a small waterproof bag and Brian our official photographer of the trip, paled as he heard this, thinking of all his valuable photographic equipment. I tried to reassure him saying that Ron was just playing it safe, but perhaps it would be a good idea for him to wrap his equipment in plastic, mainly to give him something to do. Just at that very moment Ron and Donald came back into the saloon together. Donald very dramatically said to Ron. "Patrick told me not to tell you this, but I think you ought to know, that the last catamaran I had, sank under me and I had to be rescued by the Dutch Navy." We gazed at him in amazement before falling about with laughter. It was not what we needed to reassure us at this difficult time! He never did say why he thought we ought to know about this. I can only think that seeing the approaching coast must have unhinged him momentarily because he imparted this information with an air of cheerful earnestness, as if it brought back happy memories. Nothing seemed to bother Donald and we still have visions of him standing on the end of our boom as it swung violently from side to side, trying to discover why our mainsail wouldn't reef down during one of the first gales, and being quite taken aback when told to get down.

Fortunately, the land fell away and by the time darkness came we were several miles out to sea. We read through the Pilot again and decided Santander was the next logical port to try for. At our present speed we should be off there by first light. In fact we were some 10 miles short.

We managed to contact Santander harbour pilot station

who were very helpful and gave us what directions they could to help us enter. Unfortunately, the seas were too rough for them to venture out, but they very kindly offered to meet us just inside the shelter of the harbour entrance and tow us to a mooring, as by now we had no power.

The visibility was poor, but soon we could make out the Cabot Major Lighthouse and shortly after the Isla Mauro, a small rocky Island also with a lighthouse, which sits in the centre of the entrance to the harbour. The big seas were pounding against it throwing up huge curtains of spray reaching high into the air. Very impressive. We had been instructed to leave this to starboard as we entered the harbour.

We didn't know what maneuvering we would have to do once we had entered the harbour. We brought Soñadora's head into the wind and hoisted the fully reefed main and headed towards the entrance which was by now only about a half a mile away. Dressed in our foul weather gear and life jackets we all sat out on the cabin top with David at the wheel. We were amazed to see a big trawler coming out of the harbour entrance.

The wind was blowing force 9 and the seas so big that the trawler, heaving and pitching, would disappear out of sight into the troughs of the waves, reappearing briefly on the crests, only to disappear again as she buried her bow deep into an oncoming wave as the sea crashed over her. Soñadora was riding the seas beautifully surfing down the waves like a huge surf-board not shipping any seas.

We waved to the men on the bridge of the trawler as we passed, thinking how brave they were to go after fish in these terrible conditions; In fact it soon turned around and followed us back in, we learned afterwards that it was a brand new boat going out for its first sea trials, but had wisely decided that it was too rough.

As we surfed in through the entrance to the harbour the Royal Palace on the cliffs towered over us, the wind seemed to drop as if by magic, and the seas flattened out. For the first time in days we could stand on the deck without hanging on, and talk without shouting. We found that one of the most tiring features of a storm at sea is the noise and we hadn't realised just how noisy it had been until we got into the shelter of the cliffs.

The pilot launch was there to meet us as promised, we quickly dropped our sails and the launch took our tow rope. They towed us to the front of the yacht club indicating where to drop our anchor, then cast off our towrope and departed with a friendly wave. They would not accept any payment or gifts. This was just the first of the many friendly acts and kindnesses that we were shown by the people of Santander and throughout Spain.

There was a collective sigh of relief as it suddenly dawned on us that we were now safe at anchor after the anxieties of the last few days. Celebrations were called for, but it was only 9.30 a.m. so after hoisting our yellow quarantine flag we settled for a good breakfast, and were soon tucking into large platefuls of bacon and eggs, and drinking copious amounts of tea. We had a general tidy up, stowed the sails, and all the other gear.

We located the rubber dinghy, inflated and launched it ready to row ashore. As if that had been a signal, a boatman from the yacht club arrived with a note inviting us to use their facilities and saying that they would assist us with our entry formalities when we came ashore.

Because of my damaged leg, I decided to remain aboard while Ron and the crew went ashore taking passports and yacht papers with them, to get us formally entered into Spain. As I watched them row ashore I reflected on how lucky we were to be safely anchored, having encountered all the gales and storms with no damage to any of us or the yacht, apart from myself. None of the crew had been through such dreadful weather before, and were really impressed with the feeling of safety and stable comfort that Soñadora had given us throughout, and thankfully ever since.

Soñadora, as we have said, is a Spanish word meaning Dreamer and I did wonder if having been given a Spanish name she had decided that she would like to take a look at Spain, and that was why we were here and not in Antigua. Soñadora always seemed to have a mind of her own!!

A few hours later the men returned reporting how impressed they were with the Real Club Maritimo where they had been made very welcome. The club secretary who spoke a little English had filled in the necessary forms for entry, and had issued us all with temporary membership cards, which allowed us full use of the club. Taking advantage of this, the crew had booked a table for dinner that evening in the member's dining room.

Everyone had visited the main Post Office, and had telephoned their families to the surprise of all at home, who had thought we were well on our way to Antigua!!

Ron managed to find the outboard motor buried beneath the piles of gear in the aft locker, and attached it to the back of the Avon dinghy. We remembered the last time that the Seagull outboard was used, it had been sunk by the British Navy in Dartmouth some 3 months before, but amazingly, it started with the second pull on the cord.

The yacht club was built out over the harbour on concrete piles which, at low tide revealed large black big barnacles growing on them, which would cut holes in our dinghy, but now we had the use of our Seagull outboard, we would be able to take our dinghy around into 'Puerto Chico,' which was the old fishing harbour, now used as part of the marina by the yacht club.

Yacht clubs in Spain are very much more formal than our average British yacht club. To become a member was very difficult. Members had to put down the names of their children as soon as they were born, and the fees were very expensive.

We felt obliged to keep the British flag flying, by dressing as presentably as possible for dinner, I even washed my hair, but needless to say when the time came for us to go ashore it was raining heavily, and we were dripping wet when we arrived in the large and impressive foyer of the yacht Club. The doorman looked bemused as I emerged from my wet weather gear, rolling down my long evening skirt as I stepped out of my trousers, exchanging, my boots for high heeled shoes, limping with one stiff leg into the ladies room to repair the damage to my hair. I hope he thought it was like a frog, turning into a princess and not the other way round!

I was looking forward to having a meal which I hadn't cooked myself, but they dine very late in Spain it was 9pm before we sat down to dinner. Fortunately, it was a superb meal, well worth waiting for. While waiting at the bar before dinner, we met Jaime and his English wife Angela. He was an importer of yachts and equipment and proved to be a great help to us. Whilst having dinner we discussed our plans as time was getting short for Patrick who had to be in Antigua in early December. The rest of the crew had a time limit.

Ron and I were more than ever convinced that good reliable engine power was essential, and would be even more so because when the crew left, we would have to manage on our own. We had been lucky in this case, but we couldn't always rely on a friendly Pilot boat to tow us in! Having talked to Jaime it seemed that Santander was a perfect place to put our problems right, there were plenty of engineering facilities and several ship building firms in the area.

We came to the sad conclusion that the crew would fly home. It was a subdued crew that returned to Soñadora that night, although we all knew we had made the only possible decision. And to confirm it, the next morning the weather forecast was still giving force 9 south westerly's for the 'Biscay' area and there would have been no chance of our getting away from Santander under sail with no engines.

We all went ashore and split up to go our various ways, Ron with Jaime to see if we could arrange to get on the slip in the fishing harbour, the crew to arrange their flights home. I went into the club to ask the secretary to direct me to the market, a member of the club who was with him, kindly insisted on driving me there. Fortunately, it wasn't far, for by the time I had returned to the club walking back along the promenade carrying two bags of fresh vegetables and bread, both of which are excellent in Spain, my leg was quite painful, I decided that I must consult a Doctor soon.

On enquiry, the Secretary recommended a doctor and kindly took me to visit him after lunch. After examining my leg the Doctor confirmed that I had torn a knee ligament, suggesting that he put my leg in a full length plaster of paris.

Trying hard not to laugh, I explained with the help of a Spanish/English dictionary that it would be an impossible thing to cope with on a boat. In the end he prescribed an elastic knee bandage and some pain killing tablets. I only wanted to have my diagnosis confirmed for I knew as long as I held it stiff while walking, it would heal in its own time, it eventually took three months and has never given me any trouble since.

We all met up in the bar at the club late afternoon, and all had been successful in their missions. Ron and Jaime had arranged for a workboat to tow Soñadora around to the fishing harbour later in the week, where we would be hauled out. The crew had found that Santander Airport was shut due to work on the runway, but had booked flights from Bilbao in two days time.

When we went back onboard that afternoon, someone, and we are not going to say who tied the dinghy to the stern with what is called a 'Highwayman's Knot', (one that easily undoes itself). A few moments later we looked out to see our dinghy, quietly floating away. We were just preparing to throw the knot specialist overboard to retrieve it, when fortunately we managed to attract the attention of a fisherman in a small rowing boat some way off and by much shouting and waving of arms, conveyed our request to him. He took off after it, rowing like a true "Oxford Blue".

A tug must also have seen the dingy floating away because

it altered course and snatched it almost from under the fisherman's nose, much to his annoyance, and laughingly returned it to us without claiming salvage! The fisherman who had rowed a good 200 yards to the rescue, looked quite dejected, but cheered up when we called him over to give him some American cigarettes. The Spanish seemed to like more than the local cigarettes which smelt terrible.

Later that day, another of the crew who shall also be nameless, went ashore. Later we saw him rowing back and when we asked him what was wrong with the outboard he said he had lost the petrol tap. It's easy to lose the cap off the petrol tank, but it must take a special genius to lose the tap!

That evening Jaime and Angela came aboard for dinner, we had a relaxed evening enjoyed by everyone. Gallantly, Angela invited all seven of us to their flat the following evening for 'Paella' a typical delicious Spanish dish, and chicken for Ron who can't stand shellfish of any kind.

The following day, Terry having volunteered, to row ashore for some fresh bread, returned with a fairly large fish, which he said had literally leapt into the dinghy. He was all set to have it cooked fresh for breakfast, but we managed to dissuade him by arguing that any fish daft enough to leap into a boat must have something wrong with it. It probably would have been ok, but we had not been there long enough to know what the state of the sea water was.

On the morning of the crew's departure we saw them into the taxi that was to take them to the train for Bilbao. We all felt quite sad at parting in this manner, not as yet having achieved our aims, but with the hope that we would all meet up again one day. Under very difficult circumstances we had got on very well together, which is not always the case.

That summer Donald had sailed his own yacht down from

France and had left it in Bilbao. He was returning to Spain in the Spring to continue his trip, so we were reasonably sure to see him again, but didn't know when we would meet the others. After they had all left, I suddenly realised that even though we had got a professional photographer on board, no pictures had been taken, not even a group photograph. It quite upset me. I guess so much had happened or not happened that taking pictures was the last thing on our minds. It would have been different today everybody would have been clicking away on their various mobile devices.

The day after the crew had left; the pilot boat arrived to tow us to the fishing harbour as planned. They decided the easiest way to move Soñadora was to raft up to the work boat giving them better control. As soon as they had done this, we lifted the anchor and got underway. The two men on the workboat were Chi-Chi, the yards works manager, and Miguel his brother-in-law who could speak a little English. He had worked aboard a Danish ship for some years, where he had met his Danish wife Karen, who had been the radio officer on board.

We entered Puerto Pesquero, and straight ahead of us was a wide expanse of concrete sloping down into the water, with four sets of steel railway lines carrying large steel slipping cradles, two of which had large fishing trawlers on, high out of the water. We headed towards the clear area of concrete between the two empty slips to the left, going as fast as the little work boat could take us, we tried to get them to slow down, but to no avail, they didn't realise how much deeper in the water we were to them, we hit the concrete still travelling at about 5 knots; we shot up the slope and came to a grinding halt with the work boat still trying to go full ahead and a puzzled Chi-Chi still holding onto the tiller! It was obvious we weren't going any further that night. It was on the top of the highest spring tide, our travel up the concrete had put our water-line 6 inches out of the water, thank goodness the keels had 1 inch thick steel shoes on their full 12 foot length.

Puerto Pesquero (Starboard side)

The workboat was untied and went away. We stayed aboard until the receding tide allowed Miguel to put up a ladder to our foredeck for us to get ashore.

While all this had been going on I had of course, been limping stiff legged up and down the deck. Ron had noticed Jose, one of the workman ashore assisting Miguel, also limping in the same sort of fashion, and said to me "Look you and he are a matched pair, perhaps we can turn you into a music hall act!" when we got to know them better we found that they had been having a

Puerto Pesquero (Port side)

similar joke in reverse! We found the Spanish have a very good sense of humour.

The yardmen finished work at 7 o'clock and it was their practice to adjourn to a local bar for a few drinks, before going home. As they were leaving Miguel called, inviting us to join them. We were soon in a bar called La Campa sampling the local beer and wine while getting to know everybody. They seemed pleased to have a British yacht in their yard for the first time and their open hearted friendliness, then, was just what we needed.

As we left to go back to the boat, Miguel asked me if there was anything I required, the only thing we really needed was bread and milk. The tide was well out when we returned, the flood lights of the yard were on, Soñadora lit up looking like a white swan stranded in a sea of muddy concrete. We climbed up the ladder, and went to bed feeling much more confident of our situation.

When we awoke in the morning we found a fresh loaf of bread, and a sealed plastic bag of milk, on the deck at the top of the ladder, the first time we had seen milk packaged in this way.

The men were hard at work cleaning and anti-fouling the trawlers on the slip. The tide had receded enough for us to walk around Soñadora checking the keels were ok. Chi Chi had already run the two empty cradles down below the level of Soñadora having attached a large steel hawser behind and between the two keels, he signaled, to the men in the cinching sheds at the top of the yard to start cinching in, and slowly and steadily Soñadora was dragged up until her stern was several yards above the highest spring tide mark. The steel shoes fitted to the bottom of her keels were doing a sterling service!

Ron soon had us connected up to the main electricity supply, and arranged a water hose to fill our tanks. Fortunately, one of our three toilets is connected to a large holding tank that is chemically treated. It has an electric flushing system, which we had fitted especially for use in marinas, and for circumstances like this when we are out of the water. This enables us to live onboard at all times, and has proved of tremendous value. We spent the rest of the day exploring the fishing harbour and its surroundings.

The harbour is always a busy bustling place full of interest. Outside the yard at the top were some big engineering shops that build fishing trawlers. Looking from the top of the yard towards the entrance of the harbour, a road runs along the right hand side towards the fish market, where the trawlers unload their catch for auction while the women are sorting and packing them.

Along, the right hand side of this road runs a long low building split into individual storage rooms, where the fishermen store their gear and nets. There are always men and women in front of this building repairing their nets chatting, and laughing together. It is a very happy and tranquil sight we always got a cheerful "Buenos" as we passed by. Combined with the fish market is a Bar and Restaurant called La Lonca famous for its fish dishes it is always full of fishermen and people from the market, night and day.

Overlooking the harbour are large blocks of flats where most of the fishermen live with all the shops and bars underneath. We noticed in Spain that people live in their towns and cities making them much more alive and safer. Not like our cities where the people migrate out to the suburbs at night leaving the city centre's dead.

The other side of the harbour was an open area where a travelling fair is set up for a few weeks in the spring, but was now empty. Further over were some ugly old square blocks of terraced houses and also another restaurant where people dined outside. In the spring when the wind was in the right direction, we were often tantalized by the smells of barbecued food. To the left of the houses, were the wharfs of the docks and all their warehouses, the big cranes towering overhead, which ran for half a mile curving around back towards the modern Ferry Terminal where the ferries to Plymouth and France arrived and departed. The very pretty florid promenade runs along the sea front for a good mile well past the yacht club and like all Spanish towns had plenty of tree shaded seating areas. Santander is a very interesting city.

Later that afternoon Miguel asked us would we like to have dinner with them at their 'pi-so' we were somewhat taken aback until he explained that a pi-so was a flat! We gladly accepted. Miguel arranged to meet us in the La Campa bar at 7.30pm. This turned out to be a marathon drinking affair.

After introducing us to his wife Karen who spoke very good English, and his sister Angelina, Chi-Chi's wife, we settled down to have a few drinks. After a while the girls went to their pi-so to cook the dinner while we went on a tour of the local bars, dinner not being ready until 10pm really one should get into training before going for a night out with the Spanish. Ron said it reminded him of a notice in a pub in Yorkshire which witnessed to the fact that a customer drank 11 pints while the clock struck eleven, in preparation for his attempt on the record of 12 pints while the clock struck twelve which he accomplished the following hour! Such a citizen would stand some chance with the Spaniards, but not ordinary people like us, though we did just manage to hold our own. Dinner was a fine affair which put new life into us, much needed as the wine was still flowing I don't remember climbing the ladder to get back on board. We were just alive when we awoke at 11am the following day with terrible hangovers!

Chi-Chi and Miguel we could see were working hard as usual. We later learnt that this was a relatively normal evening for them. Their day starts at 7am. A siesta from 12 to 3pm which in Northern Spain most men seem to spend it in the bar. They continue to work from 3 to 7pm then it's back to the bar until 10 pm. It's a common sight to see the wives bring the children down to the bar in their pajamas to kiss Papa goodnight. The women seem to follow a similar pattern during the day, patronizing the cafes instead of bars, and drinking coffee.

Ron took an outdrive unit to an engineering shop accompanied by Jaime to act as interpreter to see if they had any ideas to make them viable, but as they stripped it down, it became apparent from the expression on their faces and the amount of rapid conversation between them all, ending with arms being thrown up in the air, that it was hopeless. Jaime's translation of their conversation was polite but not complimentary to this example of British engineering.

Terry had thought the best way round the problem was to fit hydraulic drives, and was going to send us information on them, but Ron wasn't very keen on the idea.

The weather was so miserable rain and more rain, that we decided to fly home to England for Christmas, and go to the 1976 January Boat Show in London.

The last two weeks were quite hectic. We were invited out to dinner by various people, and gave several dinners on board. We booked our flight home from Bilbao for the 22nd December, Chi Chi had insisted on driving us to the airport. The night before we spent packing and making the boat secure. Miguel had already arranged for the contents of our deep freeze to be stored in a cold store.

The next morning early we set off for the airport with Chi-Chi and Angelina. It was a beautiful day, the first day without rain for a week, we felt quite comfortable leaving Soñadora in the care of our friends in the yard, so we could relax and enjoy the two hour journey to Bilbao.

It is a very pleasant run along the coastal road passing through several little fishing villages with good views of the sea, and hills and big mountains running inland. We stopped at a pretty little place called Castro Urdiales, over-looked by an ancient crumbling church on a cliff close to the harbour for coffee and pastries...

We arrived in Bilbao a typical industrial town and we had to wait to cross the river by the transporter bridge, arriving at the airport in good time, we said a grateful farewell to Chi-Chi and Angelina, and we were soon in the air, returning to the UK less than two months after leaving it.

We were asked many times how we felt about ending up in Santander instead of Antigua, I think we both felt it was a blessing in disguise. We had been through very bad weather proving Soñadora to be very sea worthy, we knew that engines were needed, and even experts can make mistakes we had been very, very lucky.

Santander was the ideal place to be for our needs.

The plane landed at Heathrow Airport. We had soon cleared through customs and caught the waiting bus to Reading train station from where we caught the train to Bristol.

The weather was bleak and cold as usual in December. It was obviously not going to be the Christmas in the sun we had been looking forward to, but at least we were still in one piece!

We arrived at Bristol and took a taxi to the Hole in the Wall Inn, where we had arranged to meet Ron's brother Trevor and his wife Pat, with whom we would be staying while we were in England. We paid the taxi and left our luggage in the corner of the bar while we went to telephone our Bristol friends to see if any were free to join us. David and Mona, Mike and Joyce said they would be with us in a few minutes. Returning to the bar we found we had caused a full-scale panic! The IRA had started a bombing campaign and any unattended baggage was treated with great suspicion.

The Manager was just about to evacuate the pub, we apologised for the scare we had caused, we had not realised just how serious the IRA situation was being taken. The management was glad to see the offending suitcases claimed.

Pat and Trevor had arrived and the others soon joined us. We had a very enjoyable meal, during which we regaled our captive audience with our tales of storms and terror in the Bay of Biscay, by the end of the evening I am sure they were beginning to feel the table rolling!

It was good to be home for the family Christmas and New Year with Pat, Trevor, Peter and our friends. Though we were soon fed up of explaining why we were back home so soon? I had very mixed feelings about the whole episode, very glad that the three of us, Ron, Soñadora and I, where safe with no damage, and we were extremely lucky to have ended up at Santander, where Soñadora could be sorted out.

Ron had inadvertently got his wish of wanting more time in a safe and happy environment. Santander was the perfect place for repairs, working with people he liked and trusted and we and Soñadora had, had a good realistic introduction to the sea, and had survived, and still liked the life.

While Ron went with Trevor and Pat to the Boat Show, I spent a few days with my family in Nottingham, not knowing that this would be the last time I would see my father and step mother, as they both unexpectedly died before our return five years later.

Ron spent an interesting and enjoyable day at the Boat Show making up his mind as to the type of gearboxes he would require, ordering them and all the other gear required, shafts, propellers etc. He was promised delivery to Santander by the end of February for certain. After the show they drove down to the new Forest and spent the night with Pam and Terry who put on a film show for them with his slides of the trip to Santander. Sadly I never did see them.

At the end of January we said fond farewells once again, and returned to Santander much refreshed both mentally and physically with renewed enthusiasm for the adventures ahead. We took a taxi from Bilbao Airport to the bus station, and caught a bus direct to Santander arriving at 8 am. We Called at Miguel's flat to pick up the key for Soñadora and he very kindly insisted that we stayed the night with them as there was no electricity supply on board. It was a very happy welcome back to Santander, and Spain.

Next morning returning to the yard, Soñadora was still safe and sound, but smelled musty so I opened her up to air her out while Ron reconnected the electricity supply and took on water. Santander has a heavy rainfall at this time of the year, creating a lot of damp inside, this quickly causes mildew, and it was a constant battle to keep it at bay. I found a solution of white vinegar and teak oil, quite effective for cleaning off mould and discouraging re-growth. We were fortunate that we had an electricity supply, which we could use for heating, (a dry heat) so we had no problems with condensation. I have seen some yachts that use paraffin or gas heating running with water.

Chi Chi came aboard to see that we had everything we required and invited us to dinner that night. He had his two and a half year old son Massy with him - "an amazing child." He was very intelligent you could see him working out the meaning of everything about him. If he was given a toy of any sort the first thing he would do, would be to take it apart and puzzle out how it worked. As soon as he knew he would throw it away.

This morning he picked up a hand-drill with a half-inch steel bit in it. I advised Ron to take it off him, "Oh let him have it there's no way he will dismantle that!" said Ron. Massy looked at him and walked away, a few minutes later he came back and handed it to Ron, in two pieces. The expression on Ron's face was laughable. Massy also had the painful habit of biting you to gain attention, you would feel pain in your calf, and looking down would find a small boy attached to you. Also, they had a large dog, and it was the only family I know where they had to protect the dog from the child!

However, in spite of all his activities he was a most lovable boy. Five years later, on our return to Santander with Soñadora he was running along the quay shouting Carole! Carole! He had not forgotten us.

The next few weeks we worked hard removing the old outdrive systems and cutting out the water tight compartments which had been built into the hulls to allow the outdrives to be retracted up into the hulls to reduce the   drag while under sail. Having done this we modified the hulls to accept the mountings for the prop shafts now connecting with the new gear box/engine positions. Then we had to reconstruct the hull with GRP, to do this we had to obtain the necessary materials locally, this led to many hilarious moments with language problems. The Spanish are very helpful and enter into the spirit of a guessing game with real enthusiasm. I can still remember one ironmongery shop where we brought the entire establishment to a standstill with hysterical laughter; from Ron's demonstration of trying to buy a round file. The Spanish have a very basic open sense of fun.

The customers and staff were making rude gestures to each other, though we usually managed to get what was required. If they didn't have what we wanted they would take us to another shop, often streets away. I would like to think we would do the same for a foreigner in Britain. We also had a lot of work to do inside the boat, time just flashed by.

Early one morning Miguel banged on the hulls and asked if I could render first aid to Jose. A small 20-foot motor boat had slipped off a jack when he was chocking it up and had pinned him underneath. I did what I could while they jacked the boat off him. Fortunately, there was no obvious injury but I advised that he should be taken to the hospital for X-rays. I was astounded to learn later that the nurses had complained to him about his dirty state, I don't know what else they could expect, when, the poor chap had been pinned under a dirty boat in inches of black oily mud!

Poor Jose was the most accident prone person in the yard; the injury causing his stiff leg had happened when he had tripped on the pavement and precipitated himself into the path of a fast-moving car. On another occasion a gypsy arguing in a bar with a companion drew a knife to stab him, missed and stabbed Jose instead. If anyone was hurt in the yard you could guarantee it would be Jose.

Our social life and circle of friends seemed to increase by leaps and bounds and we were befriended, helped, and entertained by people from all walks of life. One chap named Pedro, working on a little boat alongside us would take his morning break with us attempting to teach us Spanish. Funnily enough even though he couldn't speak much English we found we learnt more Spanish from him than anyone else. Most of our friends could speak a little English and were keen to improve it. Which didn't help our Spanish!

Soñadora was of great interest to the local people many had never seen a big catamaran and we were asked many times if they could look over her. One enterprising young boy aged about 10/12years, having been shown over, asked if he could bring some friends, and from then on would arrive with small parties of children for a conducted tour, making them take their shoes off and thank us very politely as they left. We think he must have had quite a good business going. On the day we were being re-launched he rushed up to Ron and shyly thrust a small purse into his hand as a farewell gift running away quickly. We were very touched and full of admiration for his extra enterprising skills.

On another occasion we were surprised to be addressed in perfect English by a man with a slight Canadian accent he told us he had a yacht in 'Puerto Chico' and we assumed he was a fellow countryman. In fact after further conversation he turned out to be Spain's leading heart surgeon, Carlos Duran. He had an English wife Estelle, whom we later met. Carlos invited me to visit the very modern Valdecilla Hospital. I was thrilled; this would be the first non English speaking hospital that I had visited, having worked as a theatre sister in England, Australia and New Zealand. I was very impressed with the highly efficient, but relaxed informal atmosphere in the theatres. I was invited to stay and watch some open-heart surgery. Again a new experience for me. It was a pleasure to see how everyone worked efficiently together as a team from Carlos down to the most junior nurse and theatre technician. The quietly piped music adding to the calm atmosphere. Music in theatres, was a new venture in the UK. It was a wonderful experience; I would have loved to have worked there.

March came and still no sign of our gearboxes etc., which had been promised faithfully for the end of February. Ron contacted Trevor to ask him to chase up the two firms concerned. Ron had gone into the method of delivery when he had ordered and paid for the gear, back in early January. It had been arranged that they would put it on the Santander ferry at Plymouth for us to collect. It was impossible to think that anything could go wrong with such a simple arrangement. However, it took another 6 weeks of letter writing, and phone calls before we finally received the goods, by this time it was May and we had to employ an import agent to help us. They managed to trace the consignment from one firm all around Europe before finally obtaining it. The other firm after insisting that they had dispatched the goods as arranged in February, admitted they hadn't sent them, and air freighted it to us at vast expense, insisting Trevor paid in advance. When it arrived we found that they had sent it COD (cash on delivery) and it was to take us months to obtain a refund. Ever since we had left Britain the UK pound had been going steadily downhill and had lost about 25%, of its value abroad. We decided that as we would be spending more time in Spain some of our money would be better in pesetas. We had scarcely arranged this, when the peseta was promptly devalued! That's life!

Donald and his wife Robbie had driven over in April to Bilbao to prepare their yacht Froya for their summer cruise with their family. They had decided it would be more convenient to sail her to Santander where she could be slipped more easily for anti-fouling etc. We went to Bilbao to help them to sail her down. However in total contrast to the last time we were in the Bay of Biscay, it was flat calm and we had to motor all the way.

We anchored outside the Yacht Club again, and when the tide was right the following day they were slipped alongside us for a week. We used to meet on one yacht or the other in the evenings for sundowners.

On their last night on the slip I invited them for dinner. Ron was on board Froya helping Donald with his engine when they heard a loud bang and looking out they were just in time to see the galley hatch off Soñadora descending from a great height, seconds later they saw me emerge looking bemused, I gave them a faint wave. They gathered from all the evidence that I had blown myself up, and they were quite right!!

Froya slipped alongside Soñadora April 1976

Up until now I had always cooked with electricity, and although having been lectured at great length by Ron on the dangers of gas in a boat, I was guilty of doing one of the things he had warned me against. The oven had a separate tap, as well as a thermostat I had got into the habit when wanting to keep food warm of turning the flame down by using the tap as I would to simmer a saucepan on the top rings, instead of relying on the thermostat. On this occasion having turned down the flame it must have blown out when I shut the oven door. Opening the oven sometime later, I discovered the flame was out, and without thinking struck a match to relight it. The next thing I knew I was picking myself up outside the galley where I had been blown, some ten feet! My first thought was to let Ron know that I was still in one piece; I had visions of him rushing down the vertical ladder from Froya, slipping and breaking a limb. Apparently, the sight of me was anything but reassuring. Luckily the hatch was not locked or hinged down, so the blast escaped upwards, or I could have been seriously hurt. As it was the injuries were mostly cosmetic with a few bruises. My eyelashes and brows had disappeared, the front of my hair was singed to an inch from my head, and my face was bright red like a boiled lobster.

Ron rushed down to the galley to make sure everything was safe while Robbie fetched me a cold wet flannel for my face, which I kept, covered for an hour until the pain had gone and fortunately no blistering occurred. The real casualty was a bowl of custard; it was plastered all over the galley. We found the most suitable form of fuel for cooking and heating on a boat was propane gas which we used and think it is as safe as any, providing the installation is carried out correctly, and the boat and the operator survive the first explosion! One of the most horrific accidents we heard of was to a girl Cordon Bleu cook on a large charter yacht in the Caribbean, who had set her clothes on fire while using a spirit stove oven though it is alleged to be the safest fuel.

Once we had all recovered from this excitement we settled down to a very enjoyable dinner, minus the custard! The following morning Froya was re-launched and anchored off Club Maritimio again. Donald and Robbie departed for the UK leaving Froya in our care until their return in July. Shortly after they had left, we had another frightening experience. Miguel, Karen and their nine month old son 'Pussa' had moved into a large old villa on the outskirts of Santander.

This villa had been empty since the owner had died 17

years before, because 'the heirs'could not agree what to do with the property. Miguel had been offered the place rent free in return for looking after it. It looked like something out of a 'Dracula' horror film; with a large flight of stone steps leading up to a pillared entrance, flanked by two stone lions, the crumbling stonework ran up the three stories to the turreted roof. One expected to see vampire bats emerge at any moment. The villa was set in a large over-run garden like a jungle with dark sinister evergreen trees breaking through. It was very dark as we said goodnight at the top of the steps. We were halfway down the steps when we were stopped in our tracks by the most horrible high pitched scream, I have ever heard, followed by a thump thump thump of something bouncing down the steps. We were riveted to the spot as it passed us, I looked down expecting to see at the very least a disembodied head, but it turned out to be the baby 'Pussa' in his baby walking frame. He had shot out of the front door at high speed and down the steps. Fortunately, without hurting himself. It was Karen's scream that caused the fright when she saw Pussa disappearing down the steps.   Ron said he had heard about hair standing on end with fright, but it was the first time he had experienced it. We had to return inside to have a few stiff brandies before we were in a fit state to go home.

Ron was to have another disturbing experience in this same garden. When Miguel had tamed the garden somewhat, they put on a barbecue to which we were invited. It was only after Ron had praised Miguel for his excellent steak that Miguel informed Ron that he had been eating horse meat. Ron spent the rest of his time in Spain poking suspiciously at any meat offered to him! He quite embarrassed me sometimes when we were invited out by requesting a breakdown of the menu to ensure there were no, what he calls 'nasty's' in it. These being shellfish, horse meat and dog amongst other things.

One evening we happened to call in at the La-Lonca bar and heard three men singing happily away harmonising in what we assumed to be Spanish folk songs. We couldn't resist the invitation to join in, and it soon felt like a Welsh pub at closing time, I felt quite homesick. One thing led to another and we found ourselves in the restaurant upstairs having a very delicious meal. We discovered they were members of the Yacht Club, so naturally we invited them back to Soñadora for a night cap. We were still going strong at 4 am when they finally left. One poor chap has lost his legs to such an extent that he was having difficulty negotiating the ladder so to be on the safe side we tied a rope around him and amidst much laughter slowly and gently lowered him down the ladder to the ground, a 15 foot drop. Fortunately, we were the only ones living onboard on their Yacht/Fishing Boats in the yard. So we disturbed no-one.

The La Lonca Bar was at the far end of the harbour—right side 1976

Our three months of heavy training in Spain now found us able to hold our own with the locals in the consumption of alcohol, but we were very glad we were not far from our bunks that night. The next day one of them returned with a dozen red roses for me a lovely, thoughtful surprise.

We had other good evenings with them before we left. We were sad to learn on our return to Santander 5 years later that one of them had been killed in a road accident.

From the end of April the weather was really beautiful, enabling us to make good progress of the work inside and out on Soñadora, and by the end of June the new drive systems were installed, and we were now only waiting for Trevor and Pat who had arranged to join us in mid-July for the trip down the coast of Spain and Portugal.

We were still leading a hectic social life as well as taking every opportunity to see the surrounding countryside, which is beautiful, hilly and mountainous with many fertile valleys, streams and rivers. Some rivers are very good for fishing. We also visited the caves of Altamira famous for their prehistoric paintings, some of them on the low roofs of the caves. Owing to damage being caused by the breath of thousands of visitors they have since been closed to the public, so we were lucky to see them when we did.

July saw the return of Donald and Robbie. They drove out in their car loaded down with gear and supplies, but had kindly found room for some stores for us as well. They had a week to get Froya ready before being joined by their children. Trevor and Pat were due to arrive in two days so we decided it was time to get Soñadora floating again ready for their arrival. We didn't anticipate any problems with this, Chi Chi said they would use the two slips in much the same way as when they had pulled Soñadora out, only this time the weight of the slips plus the trawlers would help drag us down the concrete into the water. However, this didn't work as there wasn't enough weight to move us, so we tried laying out a large anchor and winching ourselves back, but we stayed put as the anchor came to meet us!

We were still out of the water when the time came to collect Pat and Trevor from Bilbao airport. They came through immigration loaded down with 10lbs of bacon for us, which would have taken some explaining if they had been searched! Carlos had very kindly lent us his Land Rover to collect them; we had a very enjoyable trip both ways, wonderfully capped by having dinner with Estelle and Carlos that evening.

The next day still found us with the problem of getting Soñadora back into the water. By the afternoon after many different attempts we still hadn't managed to move her and we were beginning to despair when suddenly two huge earth moving machines arrived and to our astonishment attached themselves to the hawsers around the keels of Soñadora and to the loud cheers of everyone, pulled her with no effort down the slip where she would float at high tide. Before we realised what was happening they had unhooked and disappeared rapidly in the direction from which they had come. We found out later they came by courtesy of Senor Santiago Fiochi Gil, whom we had met when we first arrived he had asked his staff to look out for Soñadora. Apparently, he had realised that we were not going to get back into the water as easily as we had thought. At this time he had to go into hospital, but had very kindly remembered to leave instructions with his workmen to keep their eye on us and help us out when necessary. A most extraordinary kind thought when he had his own health problems to think about.

Stareboard side

Heavy duty earth moving machines compliments of Senor Santiago Fiochi Gil
aft Port and Starboard aft of each hull

Port side

As soon as we floated that night we motored around and anchored in front of the yacht club. That evening we had organised with Karen and Miguel a farewell barbecue at the villa (Ron insisting on providing the meat!) Many of our Spanish friends were there and also Donald and Robbie. The weather was perfect, it was a great evening enjoyed by everyone including little Massy who unknown to us had been sampling any unguarded glass getting slightly tipsy!

The following day we had invited as many of our friends as possible to come for a sail, while we tried out our new drive installations, which thank goodness proved to be very successful.

From top left to right, Chichi - Black Shirt, Ron - Pink Shirt, Miguel - Blue Shirt, Carole, Karen, Pat, Pusa, Juan and Family left side

The weather was beautiful and with about 20 people on board we made for the open sea. We hoisted the sails although there was very little wind, but it was great to feel Soñadora come alive again as her bows lifted to the swell of the open sea. We motor sailed along the coast for a couple of hours passing close to the golden beach of Sardinero crowded with its happy holiday makers before returning to the harbour.

Nobody wanted to go ashore yet, so we decided to explore the Rio del Astillero (Shipbuilders River) motoring up past the airport and the ship building yards, mostly used now for ship breaking. In fact there was one very large tanker that had gone aground before it could reach the yards, it looked like they would have to break it up where it was. We continued on up, until stopped by a road bridge, where we dropped anchor and had tea and sandwiches on the foredeck. The children on board enjoyed diving off the bows into the water, and we relaxed for a couple of hours before returning down river and anchoring off the yacht club. A good time was had by all.

The following morning we filled up with diesel and water, and then went ashore to the market for fresh provisions and other last minute necessities. This was also the last time that Ron had his hair professionally cut. Since then like most yachting couples I have cut it. After a long passage I try and cut it a couple of days before landfall "to allow the cuts to heal" as Ron painfully puts it. After making our fond farewells to all at the yacht club, and the ship yard we rowed back to Soñadora, pulled the dingy aboard, and raised the anchor and waving a final sad goodbye, motoring out of the harbour hoisting the sails as we went.

Soñadora coming alive as she lifts her bows to meet the oncoming
swell of the waves, sliding down the crest of them to rise again - a
very soothing motion

Saloon

Left to right - Carole, Trevor, Pat, Peter, Mother and Ron

Dinner is served M'lud

Double and single

Cabins en-suite

The

Galley

It was Saturday 24th July 1976. We had spent a very pleasant, happy, extremely useful 9 months in Santander, not only had Ron taught himself the basics of astro-navigation, but Soñadora now had a hot water system run off the diesel engines, and two reliable drive systems, but also much more of the interior finished.

We had made many lasting friendships and had learned much more about living with people of other races.

The harbour was crowded with yachts and sailing dinghies and the juniors were racing in their little 'Optimists' as we made for the harbour entrance and the open sea, passing the Royal Palace to port. Ron set the auto-Pilot to almost due west to sail along the coast, trimmed the sails to take advantage of what little wind there was, and settled down to enjoy our first sail under our own command. We couldn't have had better weather light winds 7 to 10 knots and small seas; the sun was shining and hardly a cloud in the sky. It was a terrific feeling to be at sea again.

A month before, Miguel had left his job at the yard and shipped aboard one of the large Santander tugs and we knew the tug was towing a vessel back to Santander from Gijon, so 20 miles down the coast, we saw the tug emerge over the horizon and we contacted them on our VHF radio so we were able to say our goodbyes to Miguel and thank him once again for all the help he had given us.

We were only two miles off the coast, where the last time we had sailed that way, the seas had been crashing up the cliffs and we were in danger of being wrecked! But circumstances were very different now. As the big red sun set we sat in the cockpit enjoying a traditional sundowner. The wind had dropped completely and we were now motoring slowly under one engine, the lack of which we had felt so keenly the previous November.

Trevor was really enjoying himself; he was currently doing his Yacht Masters Course so was keen to get plenty of coastal navigation practice. He was busy taking compass bearings and charting our position, as he did, for the rest of the trip. We had dinner in the saloon returning to the cockpit to enjoy the balmy evening under the stars talking late into the night. The rest of the night was divided into watches two on, two off. Ron and I taking the first watch. It was a perfect first night at sea.

Morning dawned on another beautiful day, we breakfasted in the cockpit after which we were able to set the sails and turn the engine off. It's comforting to have engines, but it is a great relief to be able to stop them down. We were bound for the fishing port of Luarco, and arrived off the entrance that afternoon. From the outer harbour the inner harbour is entered by a narrow curving canal with high stonewalls either side and we certainly wouldn't have had room to turn around. There were no signals to indicate whether we should enter or not so taking a deep breath we motored into the entrance and proceeded on round the corner into the harbour.

It was wall to wall with fishing boats, but a local policeman indicated to go along side two other yachts directly ahead of us. Pat and I put out fenders on the port side and Trevor was on the aft deck ready to hand a mooring line to a chap waiting to receive it at the stem of a Nicholson 35, as Ron gently brought Soñadora alongside.

The stern line was made fast and Ron put the engines in

Soñadora at the inner harbour Luarco North Spain 1976

neutral, and went forward to pass a line from the bow. He noticed a small cabin cruiser broadside onto us just under our bows we appeared to be creeping forward onto it. We had had trouble with the starboard gear box not coming out of forward gear sometimes when put into neutral. Ron being a man of action leapt over the pulpit onto the cabin cruiser's top too hold it off, shouting to Trevor as he did so to stop the engines.

It was a Sunday afternoon it seemed the entire population of the town was congregated around the harbour looking on with interest at our arrival.

When Trevor stopped the engines, Soñadora drifted back, Ron now found himself hanging by his fingertips from the edge of the foredeck immersed up to his knees in the dock water. We were of course, at the stem of Soñadora the first we knew of all this was a string of curses and a plaintive cry for help seeming to come from nowhere. We rushed up forward, as a stir of interest went through the onlookers. Trevor was studying the problem at some length while deciding what size rope loop to make for Ron to put his foot into assist him aboard. We gathered from Ron's rude remarks still issuing from below deck level that Trevor was taking far too long to rescue him.

His finger tips were turning white from their firm grip but fortunately with a sudden spurt we managed to get him aboard. The crowd cheered and Ron turned, took a bow staggered back to the cockpit to fortify himself with a double gin and tonic.

Sitting, in the cockpit looking up around the town it looked an enchanting little place, we had a very enjoyable evening later exploring it.

Dawn found us up and about intending to make an early start we had in fact started the engines to follow a fishing boat going out when it came to an abrupt halt in the narrow exit from the harbour completely blocking it. It had caught a large warp around its propeller. It appeared we would be there for a while, as the only divers they could get were some distance away. Time for tea.

Fortunately Stewart, a New Zealander, skipper of one of the other two yachts, offered to dive down to free it for them, which; after much difficulty and many dives he did. They were very grateful and gave him a bottle of Brandy for his troubles. He was very cold and the harbour water was not very clean so he was delighted to be offered a hot shower aboard Soñadora.

It was mid morning by the time we were at last ready to depart; our destination was Ribadao only a short distance down the coasts we had plenty of time to arrive before dark. We motored through the narrow canal and found we had quite a good breeze on the right Quarter for us; we were soon having a brisk sail, quickly overtaking Stewart in his smaller yacht.

Pat and I took advantage of the lovely weather changed into bikinis spreading ourselves on the foredeck, some of which is slatted with teak capped aluminum to allow for quick drainage if we shipped water over the bows in heavy weather. It was fascinating to lie down and look through these slats at the blue water rushing through between the hulls; we occasionally got a refreshing burst of spray up through them. This was the first good sail we had had for a year, we were enjoying it so much that we over shot the entrance to the river Ribadao sighting Foz further down the coast before realizing our error, we went about to return to Ribadao.

The river entrance is difficult to spot from-out at sea; we sailed past it yet again. Sighting a lighthouse we closed the coast to try and identify it from the description in the Pilot. Ron was just saying they ought to put a sign post on the lighthouse, when to our delight and amazement we spotted through the binoculars a large sign reading 'Tapia' , this is the only time I can remember seeing a lighthouse with its name on it! We now knew for sure where we were and anchored in the river close to Stewart who had already arrived; it was a very good anchorage with a town on either side and a small ferry running between them.

We didn't want to go ashore so we invited Stewart and his girl friend Katherine aboard for dinner. We had a very enjoyable evening. The next time we were to meet Stewart was in the Caribbean.

After a good breakfast we took our leisurely departure for Cederia, some 60 miles down the coast. The winds were once again fair and we had a brisk enjoyable sail.

As we entered the river we sighted Froya with Donald, Robbie and their two sons aboard. We dropped our sails, and motored up to Donald, we chatted for a little while and Donald told us that the anchorage wasn't very good he had dragged several times. We said we would anchor nearer the town, to his surprise motored off up the river in what he knew was the wrong direction. The river was forked with the town up the left hand fork obscured from us by a headland, for some reason we thought it was up the right hand fork.

We motored on up the wide river for about half a mile before grinding to a gentle halt, Ron quickly put the engines in reverse but it was no good we were firmly stuck in the sand. We could see the sandy bottom as the water was beautifully clear and the river banks were heavily wooded with no sign of life. So still thinking the town must be further on round the bend Ron and Trevor launched the dinghy. Waving a cheery good-bye they started the outboard and it was several seconds before they realised they were still in the same place. The tide was going out so fast the outboard could not make any progress; they got back on board and we all watched fascinated as the water rapidly disappeared, just as if someone had pulled the plug out of a bath. In no time at all Soñadora was sitting quite happily in a sea of sand, it was like being in the middle of the Sahara Desert not a drop of water in sight, an extraordinary experience.

Studying the chart again it was obvious that we were up the wrong fork of the river. We decided that it would be 4am when we floated again, this proved correct, we were awakened at 3am by the noise of the tide rushing back in, and just before 4am we bumped once or twice. As soon as we had enough water under us Ron started the engines and we motored down out of the river, anchoring near to Donald and slept until 9.30am

We went ashore after lunch for a look around and to check out the local bars. After which Ron and Trevor went off and managed to get some distilled water for the batteries. While Pat and I waited in a restaurant trying hard to drink a cup of tea made with hot milk!

That evening Donald had invited us aboard Froya for sundowners. We were just leaving when an American paddled up in a child's plastic dinghy asking if we would exchange a book with him. We stayed in our dinghy while Ron took him aboard, the poor chap had paddled nearly a mile to exchange just one book, Ron offered him some extras but he wouldn't take more than one. He and his brother were heading for the Caribbean in a 20 ft yacht they had recently bought in England. By now the water was getting a bit rough so, we towed him back to his yacht before continuing on to Donald's, where we had an enjoyable couple of hours, after which Donald headed for the open sea for a nights sail to El-Ferrol where we hoped to join them there the following day.

The next day by the time we were ready to go, fog had started to descend. Hoping it would be clearer out at sea we raised the anchor and motored out to the mouth of the river. Unfortunately, it became thicker than ever so we returned and re-anchored it was 17.00 hours before we could get away arriving at El-Ferrol at 21.00 hours anchoring in the mouth of the river near to Donald.

Donald rowed over and told us he had had a difficult trip

down, ran out of wind, becalmed, in thick fog and unable to start his engine because of a flat battery. Trevor and Ron went back with him to see what was wrong with his alternator. Pat and I were busy in the galley when suddenly Soñadora rocked violently upsetting my cutlery tray, infuriated I rushed up on deck to do battle with whoever had been so inconsiderate as to cause such a huge wash in the river. Only to discover that it was what must have been the entire Spanish navy, War ships, Submarines, and an Aircraft Carrier, heading out to sea at what seemed to be full speed! I looked around just in time to see the wave hit Froya and lay her over on her beam ends, as the wave continued to the banks it actually sank a couple of small local rowing boats. We were shocked at the Spanish Navy dumping their waste in the river as they left.

Deciding that I was outnumbered I settled for shaking my fist while holding on to wait for the tidal waves to subside. Everyone on Froya emerged looking bruised and bewildered wondering what had hit them.

The chaps had discovered that Donald's alternator had a faulty regulator which meant he would have to stay at El Ferrol to await spares. Not liking the anchorage we decided to move on. This was the last time we were to meet Froya as she never managed to catch up with us.

That night we anchored in Ria De Corme and had a very peaceful night we went ashore next morning to discover a typically relaxed Spanish fishing village. We bought some delicious fresh bread; these were the first round loaves I had seen in Spain. Leaving Ria De Corme at 13.00 hours we had a good sail to Camarinas a very pretty unspoiled place, but a bit smelly.

From there we sailed on down the coast to Bayona, our last stop in Northern Spain. It was quite crowded with yachts and we had difficulty finding a place to anchor where we could swing without fouling other yachts. Trevor was at the wheel directing Ron where to drop the anchor. After we had moved three times, dropping and lifting the anchor each time, Ron was getting quite irate; his temper was not helped by slipping down into the anchor locker badly scraping the skin off his right shin. He came into the saloon blood oozing down his leg complaining bitterly and demanding first aid. I sent him back into the cockpit not wanting blood on the saloon carpet I followed him with the first aid kit. It was quite a nasty scrape.

Being concerned about infection as the wound was close to the shin bone, I found a sachet of iodine, which I cleaned and dressed the wound with. Of course it stings!! causing Ron to complain even more loudly. I told him not to be such a baby.

On clearing up I read the instructions on the sachet discovering it should have been diluted in a bowl of water!! No wonder he complained, poor fellow. I asked him what he would like to drink, surprisingly he said tea please, but his leg healed beautifully with no infection problems! I didn't tell Ron why it had healed so well, until it had a week later thank goodness. We all had a good laugh about it.

Bayona has quite a comfortable yacht club, and a large castle overlooking the bay which has now been turned into a Parador, a state run hotel. It is a very pleasant town, popular with Spanish holiday makers, but we were horrified at the prices of seafood, twice as expensive as anywhere else we had met so far. There was also a fairground playing noisily on the foreshore.

A New Zealander in a yacht anchored close by, hailed us to ask if he could have a look over Soñadora, he arrived with a companion who upon stepping aboard handed us all a visiting card, and introduced himself as an Inventor, he was from Sweden, but now living in Spain. As far as we could gather he had been asked to leave Sweden for inventing an engine that was so economical that it posed a threat to the economy of the country! He was quite a character. We were to meet Simon, the New Zealander, again. We were also pleased to meet again the yacht Gyngle Boy. We had last seen Derek in Bristol Docks with his wife Kath, and son and daughter, who were heading towards the Med.

We had a few enjoyable days here before heading down to Leixoes in Portugal. We left Bayona early in the morning. Pat and I stayed in bed as usual. Ron woke us up to come and see dolphins off the port side, they didn't stay long, I think it was just a ruse to get us out of bed to get breakfast, which we ate in the cockpit, very pleasant. There was very little wind, so we motored most of the way and arrived at Leixoes flying our yellow Q flag for entry into Portugal in the late afternoon. This is the main port for Oporto which is further up the river, and the yacht harbour is to one side of the main harbour and very crowded. We had just managed to get ourselves secured to a mooring buoy when a yacht club official asked us to move directing us to raft alongside a small French yacht on another mooring buoy. The Frenchman was not pleased, and even though we had put out large fenders, he spent the next two hours holding us off until he was absolutely sure we could do his brand new yacht no harm. Understandable.

Gyngle Boy arrived just as the fog, came down and tied alongside another yacht close by. We saw a customs officer and a yacht club official getting into a small boat at the yacht club steps some 150 yards away. It was obvious as soon as they had cast off that the yacht club man who was trying to scull the boat using one oar over the stem, had no idea what he was doing and as the tide was now going out, they were starting to drift towards the entrance of the harbour. The customs official starting to panic seized the oar from the other man and attempted to paddle with it, which only resulted in the boat going around in circles as it drifted further towards the open sea.

We were looking on fascinated and amused, but unable to help, as our rubber dinghy was not inflated. The men were obviously beginning to panic as the fog was now beginning to thicken, we had just started to blow our dinghy up as the situation was now beginning to get serious, when to our relief we saw Derek rapidly sculling towards the drifting men like a true alongshore man. We felt like singing 'Rule Britannia' as Derek skillfully went to the rescue towing them first back to his yacht for clearance and then over to us.

The customs official was just about to climb aboard when he realised he had used up his last form on Gyngle Boy and would have to go through his ordeal again. His look of horror turned to relief as we offered to bring our papers over to the yacht club for him. He was so pleased that as we all sat around the table in the club filling out the paper work, he bought us all a drink, in contrast to when we tried to clear on leaving Portugal when we were nearly shot at!!

In the morning we walked through the town of Leixoes, which was very dreary. This was not long after the communist coup and political slogans were everywhere all over the buildings and roads, most done very professionally by what looked like stencils.

We discovered our watches were one hour ahead of local time, so we had to wait some time for the banks to open before we could obtain some Portuguese money. We then caught the local train into Oporto, which is quite a pleasant place, but not very happy; it seemed a poor country after coming from Spain. Overall, we found it quite depressing. Walking over a large bridge spanning the river, we were surprised to see the water below seething with large silvery grey fish. They seemed to be packed solid. We couldn't find out the reason for this, perhaps they were going up river to spawn like salmon.

When we returned to Soñadora Trevor and Ron stripped down the water pump on the port engine, which had given us some trouble on the way down, while Pat and I caught up on our correspondence. The following morning we motored around to the fuel dock, took on 200 litres of diesel, filled our water tanks, and departed. There was little wind so we were motoring again, but were enjoying ourselves catching fish for the first time since leaving Santander. We continued all that day and on through the night, sometimes we would have some wind and managed to sail and other times, we would be motoring. The weather was beautiful. We would occasionally see local fishing boats and had to keep a good lookout for fishing nets and pots, but most of the time it was as if we had the ocean to ourselves. During the day, the wind picked up so we decided to keep going to Sagres - just around Cape St. Vincente and the beginning of the Algarve. We had good weather and pleasant sailing all the way. It was dark when we rounded Cape St. Vincente and the wind was gusting up to force 9, as we sought the shelter of the cliffs in Sagres bay and anchored for a peaceful night.

Looking over the side in the morning the water was so beautifully clear that we could see the line to the trailing walker log which we had forgotten to take in before anchoring, had fouled around the propeller. The water was very cold we decided it was a job for later in the day when the sun had warmed up the water.

Sagres is just a small peaceful village strung along the cliff tops, there seemed to be little tourism and we had an enjoyable walk out to the lighthouse on the cape. Before returning to Soñadora we called in a bar for a drink, Ron and Trevor were manfully trying to order in Spanish, Portuguese being far too difficult, it sounds more like Russian to me. The Barman looked on with a blank face and after a little while spoke up in a broad cockney accent saying, "What you want then is two beers, a gin and tonic and a scotch", we all fell about laughing!

Back on Soñadora, the water looked so inviting, that I volunteered to remove the line from around the propeller. I dived in and came up gasping it was so cold. By the time I had freed the log

I was quite blue and glad to get out to warm up in the sun. I couldn't believe the contrast.

We moved on to Lagos 20 miles further along the coast, and anchored amongst some fishing boats, and went ashore. It seemed a noisy, crowded and dirty place. We found a bar run by English people that was very expensive, and the place seemed crowded with ex-patriots, complaining bitterly about the new regime.

Early next morning we were on our way to Alhao, again there was no wind so we were motoring and fishing. We caught five fish, which we baked in the oven in wine that evening; they were delicious. Alhao is a few miles up a waterway, rather smelly and dirty, but it had a very good market, the fruit and vegetables were excellent, we also bought some good crusty bread.

Our next port of call was Santo Antonia, our last stop in Portugal. Again the weather was very hot with no wind, and we were motoring parallel to a long stretch of golden sandy beach completely deserted. We couldn't resist it. We anchored 200 yards off. Ron and I dived overboard into the beautiful clear water and swam ashore, while Pat and Trevor followed up with the dinghy. On reaching the beach we splashed up onto the beautiful golden sands, but within seconds we realised why it was so deserted. We were viciously attacked by thousands of sand flies; their bites like red-hot needles. We turned round to rush back into the water and saw Pat and Trevor splashing water over themselves while beating a hasty retreat. It was the shortest visit we have ever made anywhere. We went on our way rubbing anti-histamine cream over ourselves. Talk about have you ever been had, but it gave us a good laugh.

Santo Antonio is a little riverside town on the river Rio Guadiana that marks the boundary between Portugal and Spain. As it was our last port in Portugal we were supposed to clear officially, so we motored up the river as far as the ferry crossing looking for a place to tie up, but there seemed to be nowhere suitable so we returned down river a little way and anchored. We got into the dinghy and rowed across to a derelict wharf, which seemed a likely place to land. Trevor and Ron had just stepped ashore and were holding the dinghy steady for us to do likewise, when a soldier complete with an automatic rifle gestured to us to get off. Ron tried to explain to him that we had to land to get clearance by showing him our papers and passports, but all to no avail. He either couldn't or wouldn't understand. Ron and Trevor thought they would ignore him and try and find his superior, and made to head up the steps. The soldier promptly raised his rifle to his shoulder and aimed it at them! Not liking this sort of welcome we decided they could keep their exit stamp and rowed back to Soñadora where we had a good dinner, and relaxed on deck with drinks while keeping an eye on the soldier as he lounged on the wharf keeping a suspicious eye on us. He was still there when darkness fell.

We had never visited Portugal before in its happier days but at this time soon after the communist takeover we found it dirty, with unsmiling people generally depressing and we were not sorry to be leaving. The tide was right at 2 a.m. for departure. We left for Huelva 50 miles down the coast having had a good sail we entered the river in the morning and motored up river to the town passing a large monument on the starboard side which commemorates Columbus sailing from here to discover America.

It was lovely to be back in Spain again among happy people the smiling Dockers indicated to us where to tie up and came over to give us a helping hand. We had a long walk along the rickety pier and into the pleasant town. Trevor and Pat's holiday was now coming to an end, and they would have to fly home within the next few days.

So our first call was to a travel agency who advised us that the nearest airport from which they could fly home was Seville and the only suitable flight was Friday morning, which they booked.

The next problem was how to get to Seville, so we retired to a cafe table in the open square and discussed it over ice cold drinks. It was now Wednesday it was possible to get a bus from here but we decided to look on the charts to see if there was somewhere more suitable further down the coast. On the way back to Soñadora we called into the port office and officially entered Spain once more, all very pleasant and easy.

Back on board we consulted the pilot and discovered that Seville is in fact a Port 54 miles up the Rio Guadalquivir a large navigable river and vessels of up to 180 meters in length with a draft of 20 feet can reach Seville. The tonnage handled there in a year was over 3 million tons. The river was entered at Bonanza 47 Miles down the coast so we left Huelva at 19.00 hours arriving in Bonanza at 02.30am.

We had just anchored and got into bed, when we were knocked up by the local Police, there was no problem, we think they just wanted a drink but as we were only interested in sleep, they had to make do with a couple of packets of cigarettes. 8 am found us on our way up the river riding the incoming tide having breakfast as we went. The sun was shining it was going to be a hot hot day. Five miles upriver on the port side we saw what looked to be a village of mud huts with reed roofs, they were complete with TV Aerials but there was no sign of life. Intriguing!

The wide muddy river slowly curved up through flat swampy uninteresting landscape. By now it was very hot and with no sea breeze to cool us we erected an awning over the cockpit, which gave us some relief. All went well for the first 10 miles when suddenly to our amazement we found ourselves aground. Ron quickly went astern managing to pull Soñadora off. This started a debate between Ron and Trevor, and they decided that as the pilot book they had was 20 years old the port must have been closed and the river allowed silt up. So we went on much more carefully observing the bends on the river and keeping a close watch on our depth sounder, even so we managed to go aground twice more. So you can imagine our amazement when emerging around a bend in the river we saw a huge cargo ship towering above the banks coming towards us. We took prompt evasive action getting as close to the shore as possible, and let it go on its way, completely baffled as to how it was going to get down the river when we had gone aground!

We continued on our way with more confidence in getting to Seville, but strange as it may seem we managed to get ourselves lost which seems incredible in a river, but having no chart we kept to what looked to be the main course of the river ignoring a smaller right hand fork we had gone 3 miles before it became obvious it was the wrong way so we had to retrace our course.

A couple of miles on up the right hand fork we had another surprise, confronting us blocking our further passage was a large lock gate, as it was now 5pm we had no hope that they would open the gates for us alone. We were just looking for a suitable place to anchor when there was a ringing of bells a flashing of green lights, and a man standing on the top of the lock waved us forward. We motored carefully into what seemed to us a huge concrete canyon, its walls towering 15 foot above our decks. It was approximately 100 foot wide and 600 foot long. We were amazed that they had opened the lock just for us and even more surprised when they told us there were no charges so we handed up some cigarettes tied in a bag at the end of our boat hook which they accepted with thanks.

We emerged from the lock straight into the docks, and motored on up with cranes and ships either side of us. In the distance to port we could see what was obviously the yacht club, with lawns reaching down to the river side and yachts tied to pontoons alongside. There was only one slight problem, between the yacht club and us was a road bridge crowded with rush hour traffic and much too low for our mast. When once again to our astonishment a bell started to ring, the traffic stopped, and the bridge started to lift as we were cheerfully waved through by the bridge keeper. Willing hands helped us tie up alongside a pontoon at the yacht club. We had arrived after a thoroughly enjoyable amazing trip.

Having made Soñadora secure Celestino, a club official who could speak English, welcomed us to Seville informing us that the airport was closed, but the airport office was open. Formalities completed we were directed to the office where we were told that Pat and Trevor would have to catch a bus at 6am to the Airport Moron? 48 kilometres away the thought of having to get up so early was a bit of a blow but a minor detail.

Returning to Soñadora we showered and changed preparing ourselves for a night on the town. We only had a few hours left of Pat and Trevor's company and we meant to make the most of it. We only had time to explore a small part of the city, but were very impressed by the beautiful and distinctive buildings, well laid out roads and wide boulevards running alongside the 'Canal De Alfonso' lined with trees, bushes and many flowers, surrounding the colorful restaurants, the outside terraces leading down to the water.

We were very pleased to find ourselves on one of these terraces later that evening under the colorful fairy lights and twinkling stars enjoying a superb meal. We took a leisurely walk home and had a final drink in the luxurious bar of the yacht club. Returning to Soñadora Pat and Trevor completed their packing it was 2.30 a.m. by the time we got to bed.

Arising bleary eyed at 5am to accompany Pat and Trevor onto the 6am coach out to Moron Airport. We said goodbye to Pat and Trevor watching sadly as their plane took off disappearing into the distance. We had an hour's wait until the coach returned to Seville. Stepping off the coach in Seville was like walking into an oven, it is surrounded by hills, and there was no breeze.

Most of the local inhabitants take their holidays at this time of year and we could understand why. We wandered back to the boat doing a little sightseeing as we went, stopping in the bar of the yacht club for a cooling drink, we met Celestino and had lunch there.

In the afternoon we had a swim in one of their two lovely pools, and went to bed early. We were up very early next morning to do our shopping before the heat of the day set in. The more we saw of Seville the more we liked it and resolved to come back again in the cooler season.

Returning to Soñadora we noticed that half 'Black Duck' (our pet name for the Avon dinghy) which we had left inflated and tied across the back pulpit was deflated. On examination Ron found a seam had come unstuck obviously effected by the heat, Celestino arrived as arranged to take me to the launderette in his car, so Ron came along as well to try and obtain some rubber adhesive and get some diesel fuel delivered.

That afternoon it was so hot again that the only thing to do was to swim in the pool and sleep in the shade with a cool drink alongside. That evening we had dinner at the yacht club where they were having a dance and cabaret of traditional Spanish dancing. Much better than the usual shows that we have seen put on for the tourists. We were sad we no longer had Pat and Trevor with us they would have enjoyed it so much.

In the cool of the early morning we did our best to repair 'Black Duck' leaving him deflated for the adhesive to harden. We had just finished when the diesel arrived in 44-gallon drums in a van. Fortunately, we had a length of old hose which enabled us to siphon it into our tanks. We spent the afternoon swimming and resting.

Later that evening we went for our last walk around the town, returning to the yacht club for farewell drinks with Celestino and other friends, who had all been very helpful and pleasant to us during our short stay. Early next morning I woke Ron with a cup of tea, we had breakfast while our water tanks were filling. As soon as these were full, Ron checked over the engines while I gave all the teak carpentry a good rub over with a mixture of 5o% teak oil white vinegar and a large spoon of lemon juice. It always looks so shinny and smells so fresh and never needs to be varnished, a great save on energy.

Celestino cast off our warps, waved us adios as we motored out into the middle of the 'Canal Alfonso' to wait for the bridge to open to and let us through.

The bells rang and the bridge started to lift, we motored over to wait by the lock with another yacht whilst a large ship cleared inward bound. We both entered the lock and were soon out into the river. The yacht was obviously in a hurry as it disappeared quickly. We continued at our economical speed of 7 knots, which we calculated would give us the best use of the tides and get us to the mouth of the river before dark. Of course, we couldn't use our autopilot in the river so we took it in turns to man the wheel. We were very glad of the shade the awning gave us, though we did occasionally get a refreshing breeze. We had liked Seville very much, but were glad to be leaving the overpowering humid heat.

The yacht seemed empty now there was only the two of us, but we would soon get used to it, because this was how it was going to be for most of the time from here on in. We travelled down the river much faster than we came up without going aground at all, we were learning new sailing techniques every day which gave me quite a boost. The trip down the river was made even more enjoyable for those of us, who imbibe, by the drink of "Sangria," a very refreshing drink made to the recipe of our good friend Senor Santiago Fiochi Gill, in Santander. For very hot days, as follows:

Sangria

One litre of red wine

One Litre of water

A large of glass of Brandy

Chopped lemons

Sugar to taste

A pinch of cinnamon

Plenty of ice!!

Though it was getting dark we passed Bonanza heading for Barrameda a little further on where we dropped anchor for the night and enjoyed a dinner of steak and fresh salad, relaxing with a glass of Sangria in the cockpit under the stars, while listening to some beautiful music playing on the stereo system accompanied by the soft lap, lapping of the waves passing through. It had been a very successful first day on our own.

The following day 28 miles down the coast found us in Cadiz. We dropped anchor near to three other foreign yachts. The whole quay was under reconstruction, including a new marina.

We prepared to go ashore inflating the 'Black Duck' for the first time since our repair. We had approximately 200 yards to row to shore and we were half way there when with a loud hiss the seam opened up again, I had to move quickly to the rear of the dinghy, which was still airtight! Just as this happened, we were passing an American in his dinghy returning from the shore to his yacht, who kindly informed us we were sinking. (Smart man), and Ron sociable as ever, stopped rowing to have a discussion with him on the subject. As I was now sitting in water and we still had some 50 yards to get to shore, I suggested they stopped talking, and start rowing again, which Ron did, while muttering something about he realised, now what the expression "Mad as a wet hen" meant!

We managed to scramble ashore without getting even wetter while dragging the dinghy up onto the quay, securing it to a bollard, leaving it to dry off. The problem of how to get back on board, was to be solved on our return. By the time we had reached the yacht clubhouse at the end of the long quay we had almost dried off. We went in, but it seemed to be deserted so we continued on into town.

Cadiz, the oldest city in Spain dating back to 1100BC and at that time had a population of about 1,000. It has steep ancient city walls rising high above the sea, which must have acted as fortifications against enemies in years gone by, but is now enhanced by pleasant gardens. We went into the old part of the town with its narrow streets flanked by high old buildings and many open squares with trees shading the park seats. Our main impression of Cadiz was the vast number of children running and playing. Laughing and shouting, their combined noise and movement reminded us of flocks of starlings gathering before migration.

Returning in the dark, Black Duck was still there nice and dry. Ron put some extra air into the good half, then to the amusement of the men fishing off the quayside, folded the deflated half back to stop the water coming in, we lowered it into the water, each taking an oar. We had an hilarious paddle back to Soñadora thanking our lucky stars the seas were calm.

The following morning as we departed for Gibralter ,we noticed that a four masted cadet training ship had come in a beautiful looking vessel. As we motored out we saw a large ship wrecked high up on some rocks in the middle of the bay. It must have gone on at full speed to end up there!

The Cadet Training Ship, Cadiz 1976

There was no wind and we had just set the course when a bank of thick fog rolled in from the sea. Hoping it was purely local and would lift as we got further out to sea, we continued on, but within the hour it had got thicker. Ron standing in the cockpit could barely see me on the bow as I kept lookout for any nearby ships. Ron would stop the engines every five minutes to listen to their fog horns booming eerily through the fog as we tried to identify the direction from which they were coming. Ron then blew our fog horn, the sudden noise so close it made me jump. We hate fog, as I have said before; it is one of the most frightening things at sea, we were glad to see it lift an hour later.

We could receive Gibraltar radio clearly and were able to get understandable weather forecasts for the first time. So when we heard that there was a Levanter expected. We decided to anchor in Bolinia Bay until it had blown itself out.

A Levanter is a very strong wind that blows out through the Straits of Gibraltar and unless you have no choice, it is wise to take shelter until it has blown itself out. Quite a few people intending to take up the sailing life try to sail through the Levanter going into Gibraltar. It is so rough it puts them off for life and as a result Gibraltar is quite a good place to buy a cheap yacht.

By the time we got to Bolinia, it was blowing strongly and we had quite a rough night at anchor. So at first light we decided to moor further down the bay for better shelter. Ron had great difficulty raising the anchor and when he eventually got it up, we were surprised to find the flukes on our 65lbs Danforth anchor were bent. We could hardly believe it! We had to use our No.2 anchor at the next anchorage.

Motoring on our way, we saw what we thought at first to be a black ball bobbing up and down, then we noticed splashes and decided to change course to investigate. When we came alongside we were amazed to see that it was a man swimming. We called to him to ask if he wanted help, but he made it quite plain he was in no trouble and didn't want to be rescued. We felt quite disappointed! The extraordinary thing was that we were at least a mile off shore and it was blowing a force 8 and was the last place one would expect to find someone taking an early morning swim. We anchored in the lee of the land and found it much calmer so we settled down to a restful day of reading.

By the following morning the Levanter had blown itself out. We had a nice quiet sail along that part of the coast, where Nelson had fought and died in the battle of Trafalgar.

Soon we were passing Tarifa lighthouse, then the Punta Carnero lighthouse, we were now into the Straits of Gibraltar proper. The sun was shining, the sea was sparkling and to make the occasion complete we were accompanied by huge dolphins playing around us. Looking to starboard, there was a large tanker with a bulbous bow coming out of the Straits We could see dolphins riding its bow wave, and leaping over the bulb at the bottom of the bows really enjoying themselves.

Tarif Lighthouse/Punta Camero Lighthouse

We were making good time as Gibraltar came into view; it was easy to see why generations of seamen have fondly referred to it as 'The Rock.' It is a huge lump of rock rising abruptly 1,400 feet out of the sea into the sky, a very impressive sight. To the south of us we could see the hills of Africa looking blue through the haze. We were getting very excited; this would be our first entry into a foreign port on our own. We contacted the port authorities on our VHF who advised us to find a berth in the destroyer pens port side just around the bend. We were glad of the simple instructions. We started the motors, dropped and stowed the sails and hoisting the yellow Q flag, motored on in.

Perhaps this is a good time to explain the formalities a yacht has to go through when entering a foreign port. In theory the size of the craft makes no difference, the smallest of yachts and the largest of ships are subject to the same regulations. The first of these dates back hundreds of years and relates to the health of the

Gibraltar, The Rock with Soñadora in the Pens

vessel. In the old days, plague and other contagious diseases brought in by the ships were a real problem, so a system of quarantine was arranged with various code flags to indicate the health of the ship. A ship with no disease aboard flies a yellow flag meaning 'Q' in the International Code of Signals requesting Pratique. Which is quaintly described in Reeds Almanac as a license to hold "intercourse with the port". We had a good laugh about that.

Gibraltar Bay to the South West of the Rock

The ship first anchors in a designated quarantine area and nobody should leave or come aboard the ship until it is visited and cleared by the Port Medical Officer. The next officials to visit are the Customs who check for contraband, dutiable goods, and arrange payment on any excess. They sometimes will allow these to be sealed on board so that they cannot be used during a stay. The next officials are the Immigration who looks after the entry formalities. Normally these are all the formalities required, but in some parts of the world because of the spread of destructive pests, a representative of the Agriculture Department also visits depending from where the yacht had come from, it might be fumigated. As Soñadora was to be in the South Pacific Islands of Raratonga and Nuie she had to be fumigated against the dreaded Rhinoceros beetle which attacks and kills the coconut palms. In most countries of the world these regulations have been relaxed for private yachts, although in some places such as Fiji and South Africa they are still rigidly enforced. The 'Q' flag however, is always flown to indicate arrival from foreign parts.

As we entered the port we were treated to the odd sight of a tiny yacht being rowed out by a man sitting right up in the bow leaning back on the pulpit. He was wearing what appeared to be a red 'fez' on his head. We assumed from this that he must be a Moroccan returning to Tangiers and we hoped the weather stayed fine for him. He did look funny. We were to meet up with him in the Canary Islands where we heard his very sad story.

Soñadora moored at the Pens in Gibraltar

We motored round for a while, but the pens appeared to be choc-a-bloc, full of an assortment of craft, from fine sailing yachts to derelict barges. We were at a loss to know where to make for, when we saw an official in a smart white uniform waving to us to tie alongside a fishing boat on the end of a pen. We put out our fenders on the port side and motored gently alongside. The official and a young chap with a full beard took our warps and helped us to tie up.

The official came aboard who turned out to be the customs officer. He was soon joined by the doctor and immigration officer. We filled in the necessary forms, and the formalities were quickly completed. I offered them a cup of coffee, which they gratefully accepted. They had had a hard morning. They told us where we could find the Pier Master who collected the harbour dues and organised the berthings. They departed wishing us a happy stay in Gibraltar.

Left to right Malcolm, Rilo and Peter

The chap on the deck of the fishing vessel had been joined by a nice looking young woman and introductions were exchanged. Peter and Rilo had been in Gibraltar for some time having brought their boat named Venus down from Germany and like everyone else that we met in Gibraltar they had a fascinating tale to tell.

We had to get to the bank before it closed, so quickly went ashore. There was no one in the Pier Masters office so we continued on. It is a long walk from the pens down the causeway to the entrance into town. We passed the desalination works to our right, and to our left across the water was the ferry terminal, with the end of the airport runway just visible beyond.

We had to pass the port offices, so called in to see if there was any mail for us. There was none, but the man in the office gave us his newspaper, the first English paper we had seen in weeks. A good Spanish welcome even though Gibraltar is British, the Spanish influence is all around.

We entered the town passing through a short tunnel which is cut into the ancient wall that guarded the city, experiencing for the first time, the cosmopolitan atmosphere of Gibraltar.

As we walked up the narrow main street busy with trade, we met veiled women weaving their way through the crowds of Spanish, Moroccan, Asian and European peoples. As it happened, there was also a Russian ship in port. The Russians could easily be spotted, dressed in their almost identical old-fashioned suits. It was strange to see a typically English bobby (policeman) in shirtsleeves casually strolling amongst this throng. It gave me a warm feeling of home.

We just got to the bank in time to change our Portuguese escudos into British pounds sterling, and got a good price for them. It seemed odd to be handling British money again after a year away from home, especially as we were still in foreign parts. We called in the General Post Office, collected some mail, so decided to retire to the nearest pub to read them. It was good to sit in a British pub drinking British beer again. It is another feature of Gibraltar that though they have typical British pubs, they are not tied to the British licensing laws, which in those days were quite strict.

On our way back to Soñadora we bought some strong adhesive to repair the dinghy, and some fresh bread and stores. We were disappointed with the fruit and vegetables as they were of very poor quality, because of the closed Spanish boarder. They were mainly imported from Morocco.

Returning to the pens we met the Pier Master, Gus a pleasant helpful ex-forces man whose wife was Spanish. They had lived in Gibraltar for many years and loved it, though it was difficult for his wife as her family lived across the border. We paid our harbour dues. He advised us that we could stay where we were at the moment, but would have to move if the wind went around to the south.

Walking back along the pen we saw a Solaris Catamaran, Solaris Maiden, and spoke to the owner who was out on deck. He invited us on board for a drink and Tapas. His name was Malcolm Hudson, and during conversation it came up that he had been approached to enter the Whitbread Transatlantic Race. Was this the cat? we had been told about that had entered with an all girl crew? "Not so," Malcolm said, "I didn't trust them," Being more experienced than us, he had said "No thank you."

Malcolm had been in Gibraltar nearly a year, but he moved to Jose Banus further up the Spanish coast, into the Mediterranean for the winter. Gibraltar was wet and bleak from November to February.

That evening we invited Malcolm, Peter and Rilo aboard for drinks and learned that Rilo had not long returned from Germany where she had gone home for the birth of their son, who was at that moment sleeping soundly in his carry cot in our saloon.

Venus was an old Baltic fishing boat and they had had an, adventurous time bringing her down to Gibraltar. Apparently, lights attracted Rilo like a moth, and when left on watch at night she headed straight for them, on one occasion putting Venus on the rocks! They were staying in Gibraltar because their main engine had blown up and they were trying to find some means of replacing it.

The next day we attempted to telephone UK to let our families know we had arrived in Gibraltar and intended to stay for two weeks. It was a terrible place from which to make a telephone call. The International Exchange was situated in the Town Hall, where you gave the required number with your name to a man sitting in a little cubby hole and retired to a depressing, none too clean waiting room with a few tattered non-sound proof booths along one wall. It reminded us of British Railways at its worst. We waited three hours and then were told by the man that it was 6pm, time for him to go home and we were to come back tomorrow. We were not pleased!

When we told Malcolm about this on our return he suggested we do as he did which was to go and have dinner at the Spinning Wheel Restaurant, order dinner, and then they would put the call through. What a splendid idea! Without more ado, the three of us set forth. The Spinning Wheel was a delightful little restaurant set back in a courtyard off the main street, with some tables outside, where we sat. We arrived about 8pm. They took the number saying they would put it through, but could not promise how long it would take.

We had a delicious meal, it was a lovely balmy evening and Malcolm was keeping us well entertained with his stories of life in Gibraltar. He was in his sixties, retired and on his own. He had seen Solaris Maiden advertised for sale in Gibraltar and decided to buy her to live on, to keep boredom at bay. He seemed to be managing this quite well, occasionally running a weekly trip over to Ceuta on the African coast opposite Gibraltar, for the local British civil service personnel, sometimes going up as far as the Balearic Islands. He handled the yacht on his own without any problems. It was after midnight and a few bottles of wine later when the call finally came through.

We were pleased to hear all was well at home, but startled to learn that Sylvia and John, friends of mine who I had expected to be joining us in two week's time, were in fact flying to Malaga the following afternoon. As it was now after midnight that meant that very afternoon! There was no way we could leave immediately so they would have to book into a hotel until we arrived. We still had to take on fuel and water. We had planned to go over to Ceuta for gas and fresh stores; also Ron had to service the engines, and make a better repair on the dinghy. Suddenly, our nice leisurely fortnight was reduced to four days.

That evening Malcolm came to dinner over which he informed us that he had got an American couple wanting to go to Ceuta and would we take them as a charter. We were pleased to accept. They were going to be on the quay at seven the following morning. Fortunately, they turned out to be a very nice couple, who just wanted to get back to Madrid where they lived. He was something to do with the management of a famous American Department Store.

Because the border with Spain was shut, getting back into Spain from Gibraltar by 'normal' means, entailed catching a ferry to Tangiers, going over land to Ceuta, (a Spanish colony) catching a ferry back from Ceuta to Algeciras which is just the other side of the border from Gibraltar! By going with us direct to Ceuta they saved much time and expense.

Malcolm also had a charter party of 20 British civil service personnel wanting to go to Ceuta and suggested we follow him. He also intended to fill his gas cylinders as the cost of gas was less than half the price of that in Gibraltar, as was beer and wines. We cast off our warps and followed him out of the port calling on the VHF to notify the authorities that we were leaving, but as we had not taken on any bonded goods this was the only formality necessary.

The weather was perfect, but unfortunately there was no wind for sailing so we set the autopilot course to follow Malcolm motoring to Ceuta. Don and Sheila the American couple hadn't had breakfast and neither had we. So I set to and cooked a good egg and bacon meal which we all enjoyed. We sat on deck keeping a watchful eye on the shipping as we crossed their lanes, occasionally having to slow down to go astern of them. It takes about three hours to motor across at a comfortable speed as the morning grew hotter we all took shelter under the awning and enjoyed some refreshing ice-cold beer.

We entered the harbour and tied up to the quay behind Solaris Maiden. Don insisted on paying us £15 instead of the £10 as agreed, ignoring our protests, and also insisting on taking us out to lunch. Meanwhile Malcolm had very kindly taken our cylinders out with his to the gas works for filling. The taxi drivers were used to this and they would quote a keen price for the trip there and back including the waiting time. By doing this the taxi drivers made sure that cylinders were filled quickly. On your own, you could be waiting there for hours.

After a nice lunch we helped Don and Sheila with their luggage onto the ferry wishing them a good trip. Returning to Soñadora we found that Don had also left us a bottle of Dimple Scotch whisky. We had been fortunate with our first unexpected charter and hoped that if we ever had any more charters they would be as pleasant as Don and Sheila.

A Spanish official hailed us from the quay to take our particulars. They had a very casual attitude to entry and departure in Spain, just as long as you caused them no problems. However, they do keep a very keen eye on all yachts and can be very severe with any troublemakers. Malcolm had warned us that it was well understood it was not wise to say you had come from Gibraltar. As this official had more or less told us that we had come from Malaga, we didn't disagree with him. We paid him the harbour fee of a few pesetas, completing the formalities pleasantly in a matter of minutes.

Malcolm had returned with the gas, so we all went for a walk around the interesting town, more Spanish than African, as it is where the Spanish Army do a lot of their training. There seemed to be soldiers everywhere we looked.

We didn't want to arrive in Malaga in the dark so decided to leave Ceuta about midnight and have a night sail. Malcolm had dinner with us. His charter party straggled back more or less sober having had a good day and they departed for Gibraltar about 9pm.

It was after midnight as we left Ceuta harbour. The night was very dark and the wind was blowing from the east at 20 knots so we hoisted the sails, and set a course to cross the shipping lanes as quickly as possible intending to sail up the Spanish coast. The Straits were very busy with navigation lights everywhere, and we were on a reach sailing quite fast keeping a careful watch on all the shipping, which at times came quite close to us.

Crossing our path, was a very large container ship with it's decks piled high, outward bound for the Atlantic. Ron turned Soñadora to starboard to show his port light to the ship indicating to them our intentions to go astern of them (normal procedure).   Our speed dropped off as we almost luffed up to windward. This means losing the drive from the wind in the sails.

All at once a lamp on the bridge of the ship started to flash at us. We were not very good at Morse code, but had learned all the more urgent signals; it appeared that the ship was flashing U (...-) which means you are sailing into danger. Ron handed me the wheel and dashed into the saloon to check the chart. I looked all around, but there seemed to be nothing near us, other than the ship, which was still flashing. Ron quickly returned "There is nothing dangerous on the chart" he said, "I'll start the engines anyway," and the engines roared into life. By this time we were just clearing the stern of the ship and to our horror we could see the red and green navigation lights of another large ship bearing down directly upon us. It couldn't have been more than 150 yards away and we could see its bow wave foaming white in the dark. Ron quickly gave the engines all they had. We surged ahead and the ship passed just astern of us, its wash lifting our stern and propelling us forward violently. It must have only missed us by feet...

So far, this was the nearest we have ever been to being run down. We owe our lives entirely to the vigilance and quick action of the unknown man on the bridge of that cargo ship, who had alerted us in time to have two good engines running giving us precious time for quick action.

We often think of this when we hear some 'dyed in the wool' yachtsman extolling the virtues of cruising without engines, under sail alone. This was our second near miss with death. The ship that nearly ran us down was the Algeciras to Ceuta ferry which was very fast and if it had run us down it would have been no one's fault. We were both crossing the shipping lanes correctly, we had both gone astern of the cargo ship and by the time we had first seen him we were most probably under his bows and out of his vision. He would probably never have known that he had even hit us.

As soon as our heart rate dropped to somewhere near normal and we had realised that we were still in one piece, Ron set us back on course and stopped the engines. I went down to make a very much needed cup of tea, laced with brandy! When I came back up with the doctored tea, Soñadora was back on autopilot and Ron had the binoculars firmly attached to his eyes looking very suspiciously at every light within miles of us. This was our first night sail on our own, and our troubles were not yet over.....

The wind speed had increased to 25 knots and we were travelling at over 15 knots and were soon over to the Spanish side of the Straits. We had to alter course a few degrees, which brought us harder on the wind, so we decided to change down headsails. I went forward to catch the sail as Ron released the halyard at the mast. Just as he dropped the sail there was a loud bang and the mast and rigging shook. The boom had swung right over and hit the aft shrouds. Fortunately, Ron was at the mast or the boom would have knocked him overboard. Soñadora had no drive now and was rocking and rolling beam on to the seas. Ron dropped the mainsail quickly to stop the boom thrashing around. We now had what seemed to be acres of sail being lifted and blown around the decks by the wind.

It took us a while to get this mess sorted out and to discover what had caused the boom to break loose. This turned out to be a $3/8^{th}$ inch stainless steel shackle breaking in one of the mainsheet blocks. This was another example of badly designed yacht gear. A large block capable of handling tons that would only accept a shackle rated at half its load.

We fitted a new shackle, raised the mainsail with a reef in it hoisted a No.2 Jib. We went more quietly on our way, hoping the excitement was over for one night.

Fortunately, it was and we each managed to get a few hours sleep, while the other kept watch. We arrived off Malaga at 9 a.m. and by the time we had sorted out where we could tie up in the harbour it was 10 o'clock. Sylvia and John who had spotted us coming in from their hotel, a Parador, high above the town, were waiting to take our ropes to tie us safely to the quay bollards. We had arrived and felt surprisingly fresh after what had turned out to be a hair raising night sail, the first on our own. A very memorable trip.

J ohn and Sylvia were soon aboard with their luggage stowed and enjoying a cup of tea while Ron and I had a belated breakfast. It was lunchtime before we had caught up with all the news. They had arrived late the previous Evening, spending one night in the hotel, and had seen little of Malaga. So we decided to spend the rest of the day here for a little sight-seeing and have an early night to allow Ron and me to catch up on our sleep. In the late afternoon we had a lovely walk through the gardens overlooking the harbour from where bush and tree lined foot paths zigzagged their way up like an Alpine walk to the Parador at the top. We sat on the hotel patio enjoying a drink in the cool of the early evening while gazing out over the tranquil vista of town and harbour. It was delightful.

We were almost ready to depart next morning when George, skipper of another British yacht hailed us from the quay. We had last met on the west coast of Spain. We had seen his yacht on arrival but had found no one on board. George was having trouble with his engine, which would not start. He had spent two frustrating days trying to get someone to put it right. The local agents for that make of diesel engine were insisting that it was necessary to remove the complete engine from the boat, which was a major task. George wanted Ron to have a look and give him his opinion.

Ron found that it was a faulty starter and some three hours later had it repaired and the engine running. George was so relieved that he insisted that Ron accept a bottle of whisky and gave me a bottle of French wine. This was the second bottle of whisky Ron had been given in two days, lucky for me but unlucky for Ron who only drank gin, beer, and red wine.

It was after lunch before we left Malaga bound for Motril. The sun shone brightly but there was no wind for sailing, only flat seas for motoring. John and Sylvia were soon spread out on the foredeck sunbathing. Before long I had to warn them to come out of the sun. The combination of sun and sea quickly burns the skin.

Our late start meant that we did not arrive at Motril until after midnight, where we dropped anchor, and after checking that all was well we retired for the night.

In the morning, we could see the pontoons of a yacht club still under construction with some empty marina berths and as we intended to visit Granada and the Alhambra we went into one, mooring stern-to, this was the usual method in the Mediterranean.

We all went ashore calling into the yacht club to book in and pay our dues. The club and marina were still being built. This was 1976 when there were still only a few marinas. Jose Banus was the only one between Gibraltar and Alicante. Now there are many, and they all seem to be busy.

We discovered that the marina was a few miles away from town with no taxis and the local transport was not due for some time. We had just started to walk into town, when to our surprise John stepped out into the road, holding his hands up stopping an oncoming car. Before the startled Spanish driver realised what was happening he had four passengers. John, an extrovert sales rep. thought nothing of this, but Ron was quite embarrassed, while at the same time pleased at not having to walk. The driver good-humouredly chatted to us and we replied in our poor Spanish. We managed to convey our intention of going to Granada and he kindly dropped us at the bus station, for which we thanked him very much. It would have been quite a long walk.   Fortunately, the bus was due in half an hour so we went into a local bar for a quick drink which was served with tapas, a dish of prawns, a great Spanish tradition.

The bus journey then to Granada was a beautiful scenic ride through the mountains, with hairpin bends and precipitous drops. We passed through many olive, lemon, walnut, orange,

151

Chapter 11 Alicante and Last Visitors from Home

almonds and fig groves, all growing well. On arrival at the bus station in Granada we went directly to the Alhambra.

The Alhambra is a palatial walled citadel built on one of the hills overlooking the city of Granada. It was started in 1238 by the first of the Moorish Nazarite Kings and was added to over the years, and finally completed by Mohammed V. It was the last stronghold of Moorish rule in Spain.

It has more than thirty towers and palaces and all with beautiful mosaics, carvings, fountains, and water gardens. The sheer delicacy and beauty of it all make it one of the wonders of the World. It is far beyond my powers of description. It has to be seen to be appreciated. The whole province of Granada is beautiful and is perhaps best summed up by the poem, cut into the marble over the entrance gate of the Alcazaba, the guardian castle of the Alhambra which reads :

Give him alms women, for there is nothing in life, nothing so sad as to be blind in Granada.

The bus left for Motril at 8 0'clock. We had only had five hours to look around which was nothing like enough. I could have comfortably spent a few days there.

We had a very hair-raising trip back the driver must have been in a hurry to get back to his girl friend and obviously thought he was at the wheel of a racing car! He went flat out all the way, skidding round the bends many with sheer drops. To look out of the window and see nothing below was quite disconcerting. I was thankful to be alive when we got off in Motril, where we were lucky enough to catch a local bus back to the harbour.

The next few days were spent in leisurely cruising up the coast to Alicante, stopping every night at a different little port or harbour. The weather was superb but unfortunately there was no wind at all so we had to motor all the way. We all enjoyed ourselves very much. Though Ron and I much preferred the Atlantic coasts of Northern Spain, where with the exception of Granada, the scenery and anchorages were more beautiful and interesting and there are fewer tourists.

We arrived at Alicante at 2pm and motored through the main commercial harbour, into the large inner harbour. It was crowded with yachts of all shapes and sizes, the quay that ran along the front of the town, with large impressive buildings rising behind it. We motored slowly up and down looking for a space without success eventually having to tie up alongside a large black schooner called The Black Swan.

We later learned that it was supposed at one time to have been owned by Errol Flynn. It certainly looked the part; you could easily imagine Errol swinging from the rigging with a cutlass between his teeth. The Spanish crewman onboard wasn't very happy with our presence but it was the best we could do for the moment, we promised to move as soon as we could.

We made Soñadora secure and went ashore and we were immediately impressed by the Parque Canalejas, gardens running the full length of the front separating the town from the quay. It was very pleasant to walk through them, shaded by the many trees surrounded with flowers and shrubs. The wide pavements were laid with beautiful patterned terrazzo tiles, which though lovely to look at were very slippery when wet. There was a bandstand in the centre, but the noise of traffic rather spoilt the effect when the band played. Traffic roared along the wide streets on either side of the park. The actual front of the town was crowded with restaurants and bars, their pavement tables and awnings making a colourful splash.

Our first destination as always was to the post office which was situated in a pleasant garden square shaded by large trees where we could sit to read our mail. We were pleased to learn that Ron's elderly mother had decided to fly out and join us for two weeks, which we had hoped she would do.

That evening we telephoned Trevor to confirm -the final arrangements. John and Sylvia also confirmed their flight home on Sunday, in two days time. On the way back we walked along the quay to see if there was any space to get Soñadora stern-to the quay. The only place that looked likely was just to starboard of where we were tied at present. There was a small motor cruiser and a catamaran if they were to close up it would give us room between them and the harbour ferry. We spoke to the owners who were agreeable and arranged to move in the morning.

After dinner we all went for a walk around the town and were pleasantly surprised to find a long sandy beach only a few hundred yards north of where we were berthed. The holiday makers were mainly Spanish, with some Germans and Scandinavians instead of the expected British. A good sign, the locals always know the best places.

We walked for a little way along the beach, on returning we passed through a cluster of stalls selling all sorts of holiday bric-a-brac. For some reason John brought a small yellow plastic duck on a stick with a plastic windmill in its beak, handing it to me! It was still in my hand when we returned back on board, I casually jammed it alongside the wheel, and there it remained all the way round the world being patched and repaired as necessary, becoming one of our mascots keeping a constant watch for us. When Ron is asked who does the navigation he usually replies "I leave it to the yellow duck", and I must say his beak is usually pointing in the right direction!

Sunday morning we accompanied John and Sylvia to the airport. As we sat waiting for their flight we were surrounded by hundreds of holidaymakers queuing for their charter flights home all with varying degrees of suntan or sunburn. We were astounded to see standing next to nearly everyone a huge 3ft high toy donkey wearing a large sombrero!! This highly amused Ron who spent the time trying to decide who was in charge of who, and was quite disappointed that he was unable to get John and Sylvia one to see them home safely. I'm quite sure it must have required an extra plane to accommodate them all!

We had two weeks to wait before Ron's mother arrived. During this time we got to know the area and our neighbours on other yachts, mostly very nice people. One exception was unfortunately a resident Englishman who was unwise enough to demand a weekly fee of $1-50 off Ron for the use of the local council rubbish bins. Ron offered to deposit him in one of them for nothing and we heard no more of it. Amazingly we were told that many visiting yachts had paid him.

One morning when Ron was on deck, he glanced across at the little ferry moored alongside us, and noticed blue paint running out from its scuppers and down the topsides into the water. He saw the man on board pour diesel over the deck to clear up the paint which had spilled out of a 5 gallon drum. This also poured into the water and a large slick of blue paint soon surrounded Soñadora and other yachts down the quay. It was quite choppy in the harbour, and so it was splashing blue paint up the hulls of the yachts; a rubber dinghy tied to John's motor launch alongside us was covered in it.

The other yacht owners and Ron approached the man who pointed to two yellow lines painted on the wall of the quay and said "Anything that happened past those was nothing to do with him." They then went to the Harbour Master to complain and got no satisfaction, but one of the other yachtsmen, who knew about these things went to the local boatyard and obtained a quote for the slipping and repainting of his yacht. Then he went back to the man and told him we would all do the same and sue him for the bills. Within hours he had someone in a dinghy cleaning the paint off the yachts.

Chapter 11   Alicante and Last Visitors from Home

There was a young German couple, Walter and Ushi lodging with John on his motor launch and alongside them on the catamaran Samantha was Ron, Pauline and their two children. We would all meet from time to time for a drink and a chat; we also met the owners of two New Zealand yachts Polack and Sylvia who we were to meet again in other parts of the world. These two N.Z. yachts were the first to come through the Suez Canal after it had been reopened.

When we arrived at the airport on Sunday to meet Ron's mother as arranged, we were informed that there was an air controllers strikes and there would be at least a 6 hour delay in the arrival of her flight. We returned four hours later armed with sandwiches, coffee and books prepared for a long wait.

This was the first time Mother had left England or been on a plane. With these delays we were worried she might arrive in a distressed condition and we wanted to make sure we were there to meet her when the plane eventually arrived. A few hours later the flight arrival was announced. We waited anxiously at the barrier for her to appear.

When she arrived she was escorted by a handsome man who, was carrying her cases, He was 6ft plus and she 5ft, nothing and we had to laugh as she was chatting away to him without a care in the world. We were waving and shouting for some time before she even bothered to look around to see if we were there. You might have imagined that she had been flying all her life. She finally saw us, said goodbye to her escort, and came through the barrier to join us. It was such a relief to see her looking so well and relaxed. When we asked her how she had enjoyed her first flight, she said marvelous and couldn't understand why some people make such a fuss. She made us laugh.

It was quite dark when we arrived back at Soñadora but with me holding Mothers hand she walked the plank to board with no problems. I had prepared a cold supper before leaving which we ate while we exchanged all our news. Mother was quite excited at being back on board Soñadora after nearly a year and approved of all the finished interior work we had achieved. It was quite late when we eventually got to bed.

Mother settled down to life on board Soñadora very well. Most days I took her to the beach for a swim which she thoroughly enjoyed. She hadn't swum in years and looked very smart in her one piece bathing costume, in contrast to some of the other women holiday makers. It didn't seem to matter to them how old or fat they were, and wore what they liked even tiny bikinis without a care in the world. I thought they were wonderful.

The yachts were a great attraction to the Spanish holidaymakers, who would congregate along the quay gazing at them. We spent most of our time under the sun-awning in the cockpit at the stern, so they didn't bother us too much. Every so often though, you might be laying in the saloon having a quiet read when you would hear a clomp -clomp,- clomp, like a herd of elephants on the cabin top, you would find the whole of a Spanish family assembled around the base of the Mast, having their photographs taken! They would smile sweetly, thank you kindly and walk off leaving us open mouthed.

On one occasion Ron was disturbed during his customary siesta and shot up onto the cabin top to remonstrate, only to find himself seized, to be included in the family group photograph and then passionately kissed by the Mama of the party. Who wanted to take him home with her. It was hilarious.

After that he would check first to see who it was, before going forward to chase them off, or send me if he thought it was a big Mama there again. He wasn't taking any chances.

Mother soon got to know everybody, she accompanied us to all the parties, one of these being Ushi's birthday party, held on

Basils yacht Polack. She was intrigued with this new kind of life style, meeting people from all different nationalities in such a casual friendly manner, listening to all their stories, she thoroughly enjoyed herself. We spent some time sightseeing and exploring the city.

Alicante has a very good, large market. Mother was very impressed with the quality of the vegetables and fruits but a bit horrified at the price of meat and fish, which at that time was much more expensive than in Britain. We also spent a few interesting hours browsing through the coins and stamps at the antique market, visiting the "'Castillo Santa Barbara" the ancient castle overlooking the town and sea, with marvellous views.

The day before Mother was due to leave was Ron's birthday so I decided to bake him a cake and throw a party. It was a great success, people were dancing in the saloon and out on deck, even Mother had a few dances, and to her surprise and delight they presented her with flowers and a leather purse as a farewell gift. This was a perfect ending to her holiday she said that she could quite easily have become a permanent passenger and she would have made a good sailor, like Ron she never got sea sick.

Next day found us once again at the airport waving a sad farewell to Mother, who turned out to be our last visitor from home for four more years. My family, whom I was expecting to fly out and cruise back down to Gibraltar with us, unfortunately couldn't make it.

We had just returned back on board when to our surprise we had two unexpected visitors. Don and Sheila our erstwhile passengers to Ceuta they were on a visit to Alicante and had spotted Soñadora earlier that day, but with no one on board, had decided to call back that evening. They couldn't spend long with us having to drive back to Madrid that evening but it was good to meet them again.

Chapter 11   Alicante and Last Visitors from Home

Now it was time for us to return to Gibraltar to prepare for our trip to the Caribbean. When we announced our intention to leave in the next few days, Walter asked if we could give him a lift down to Marbella. He knew someone there who could get him a job and, Ushi for family reasons was returning to Germany.

We had intended to sail non-stop to Gibraltar but it would be no trouble to drop him off. They were very short of money and Ushi was going to have to hitchhike home. The day before we sailed Walter amazed us all by turning up with a hitch hiking companion for Ushi a black bundle of curly fur with two big eyes peering out, a lovely little poodle puppy which eagerly licked everyone in sight and promptly fell overboard, quickly being rescued. It was not at all put out by this experience it was as lively as ever. We had to find a tall box to put him in for safety, before we could all relax and have a few farewell drinks.

It was a sad scene the next morning as Walter kissed Ushi goodbye and we watched her walk away carrying her hold all in one hand, and clutching the little black puppy to her with the other. I don't think there was a dry eye. It did not seem real, or right, but there was no time to help or advise. They had not discussed their plans with any of us.

Outside the harbour the wind was blowing freshly from the South East and we were soon making good progress under sail. We had been going well for some time, but when I went forward down into the starboard shower-heads, I heard loud bangs. I quickly came back up and told Ron, on investigation he found the anchor hanging over the bow swinging on a short length of chain. As Soñadora plunged into the short choppy head seas, the anchor was knocking into the hull. By the time Ron had it on board and secured, he was soaked to the skin. We didn't know what damage it had done other than chipping the gel coat, luckily it didn't look too serious but it taught us another lesson.

Chapter 11   Alicante and Last Visitors from Home

We had become too complacent during the last few weeks of calm weather, and had got out of the habit of securing the main anchor, just leaving it stowed on the steelhead roller. From this time on we always made sure it was securely tied down as well.

We sailed all through the night, Walter and I taking the first watch, with strict instructions to wake Ron if I was in doubt about anything. We were in a reasonably busy shipping area. To be close at hand in case of emergencies, Ron invariably slept in the saloon if he was concerned when off watch at sea.

Shortly after taking over my watch I was startled to see directly ahead of me what seemed to be a large well lit city, it took me several moments to realise that this was a large liner on collision course with us. I promptly slightly changed course to starboard and as they say we soon passed 'like ships in the night', it was the Canberra on one of her Mediterranean cruises, she looked a beautiful sight all lit up but having spent more than three months of my life aboard liners while enjoying them immensely, I still wouldn't have changed places with anyone on board, there is much more satisfaction in sailing your own vessel.

This was Walters first time on a yacht and he was thoroughly enjoying himself. He made a good crewman, scrubbed the decks, took his turn washing up, took his watch and was good company. We lazed away, the next day.

It was nearly dark when we were approaching Marbella. Though we had passed it before when on our way to Malaga from Ceuta to pick up John and Sylvia, it was dark. So we had no idea of the shape of its coastline, it seemed to be all lights. Walter who had also been there a few times, but couldn't help as he had no idea what it looked like from the sea

We couldn't locate any of the light buoys shown on the chart, which should have been quick flashing. Ron headed Soñadora inshore to where he thought Marbella should be. By this time it was quite dark and we were pleased to come right up to one of the buoys. We could see the light on top that should have been flashing. It was unlit as were the lights on the harbour walls where we approached.

We didn't like what we saw and decided to go on to Jose Banus a few miles further on, where we anchored outside the marina for the night.

After a good meal we relaxed in the cockpit, it was pleasant to sit quietly looking at the lights of the marina without the noise of the engines for the first time in 40 hours. The next day, after breakfast, we slowly motored into the marina and said fair well to Walter dropping him off at the fuel jetty, when we noticed Solaris Maiden, we hailed Malcolm who came up on deck. He said he was returning to Gibraltar soon so would see us there before we left, so we continued on along the coast to Gibraltar.

This was the first time we had approached the 'Rock' from this direction and could see the openings to the galleries where in days gone by the guns had covered the approach across the isthmus towards the mainland of Spain. We passed eastern beach and the beginning of the airport runway we were soon in the shadow of the Rock, One part of the steep side overlooking Catalan bay was covered with corrugated iron sheets acres of them we were to discover later that this was the water catchment area. We were soon rounding 'Europa Point' and the lighthouse heading along the west side past the naval dockyard.

We entered the harbour again calling the harbour authorities on our VHF radio to report our arrival. Our spot alongside Venus had been taken but we found a spot on the back wall of a pen Gus and a customs man, helped us to tie up. It was Friday October 10th 1976 and good to be back in Gibraltar again.

Chapter 12   Gibraltar

Gus warned us that the weather forecast was bad, and they were expecting southerly gales. This would make our position on the back wall of the pen very uncomfortable, because the seas build up in the harbour and thunder down to the pens to crash against the back walls. On one occasion a small yacht was deposited on the quay and wrecked. However, it was so crowded here with yachts that there was nowhere else we could go, other than into the commercial docks which were very dirty.

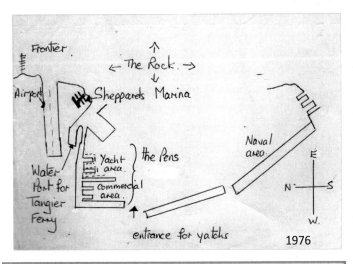

Illustration of The Pens in Gibraltar showing the Yacht area

Gus had a supply of tyres in his shed, which he kindly lent to us to help fend Soñadora off the wall. We tied them in bunches of four and hung eight bunches between our rubbing strake and the wall. By this time it was late afternoon, the promised wind had got up and the waters were quite choppy. We spent a hectic night, with Soñadora being pounded against the wall, without damage, thank goodness, the tiers doing a sterling job. The bundles of four were being quite flattened by the violence of our movement. This caused the ropes holding the tiers to chaff; we had to renew them several times throughout what seemed a long night.

This would have been a quite impossible place for a

monohull as it would have, rolled, smashing, its mast and rigging against the wall. Later in the morning we were glad to see a space become available alongside Blue Lizard an old 70 ft. MFV.

A large motor yacht that had been alongside it had left in search of quieter waters. We went aboard Blue Lizard and asked Sally and Scotty, the owners, for permission to tie to them; they agreed and stood waiting to take our lines as we came alongside. It is times like this that we are glad to have two powerful engines. With me fending the stern off the wall, Ron put one engine ahead, one engine astern and spun her bows round to face the oncoming seas, in minutes we had maneuvered alongside Blue Lizard. We were now much more comfortable with our bows facing into the incoming waves we could relax, a bit. It's bad enough having to take watches at sea without doing it in port.

Soñadora in The Pens on the back wall

Sally invited us aboard for coffee. They told us that they had also started off from Bristol in a catamaran intending to do much the same as us. They had made the mistake of trying to buck a Levanter into Gibraltar and they had unfortunately already blown out their mainsail, their only other form of engine power was their outboard, much too small in those conditions, so they called up Gibraltar Radio requesting a tow in.

As their position was nearer to Tangier's it was suggested that they contact them and get towed in there. This they did, and were astounded to see in a very short time, a large ocean going tug arrive to tow them, having been expecting something in the way of a small fishing boat. Once safely in port they were presented with a bill running into thousands of pounds. They decided this was far too much refusing to pay it and were promptly put under arrest on their own boat with an armed guard on the quay.

Their only method of battery charging now was their outboard, when they started this, the guard under the impression they were trying to make a run for it, nearly shot them, it was a very nervous time.

After that the yacht was chained and padlocked to the quay. They were only allowed ashore one at a time to obtain essential supplies,

This went on for some months without much help from the British Consulate, until they became news in the British National papers, which sufficiently disturbed the high life of the diplomatic officials there to put some pressure on in the right quarters. The suggestion was made that Scotty should make an offer to the Tangier officials of a few hundred pounds, which was quickly accepted by the authorities. Scotty made an even quicker departure to Gibraltar, sold the catamaran, and bought the Blue Lizard, which they now use as a houseboat and love the life.

Other people that start out looking for a life of adventure, are unlucky, things go very wrong, their dreams are shattered and by the time they get to Gibraltar they have had enough of the sea, selling their yacht and manage to eke out some sort of a living while they wait for their circumstances to improve.

One Old Dutch barge was being used as a boarding house, every nook and cranny rented out. Others bought and sold anything you could think of.

One chap had managed to corner all the British Navy Rum, when the British Navy stopped the traditional daily 'grog' ration; they were selling it off at a good price in the original gallon stone jars.

One of the more sad, but funny tales concerned two brothers and their wives, who had sold everything they possessed, bought a yacht, intending to see the world, but by the time the yacht had reached Gibraltar, one brother's wife had disappeared taking all their money with her, the other brothers wife had left with the other brother, leaving the remaining brother with 'sans wife' and 'sans money'!! Life was never boring in the Gibraltar Pens. Fortunately, Sally and Scotty were quite successful.

This time we intended to be in Gibraltar for five weeks to prepare Soñadora for her first ocean crossing, and to explore Gibraltar as thoroughly as we could, weather permitting. This year the weather was unusual, there had been very few Levanter's, but a lot of strong winds coming in from the West and South making Gibraltar cold, wet and miserable. Malcolm said that after November it was a dreadful place to be, with endless rain.

On one of the fine days we walked all around the bottom of The Rock, "Catalan Bay" on our left and the Atlantic even crossing the airport runway to look at the closed border gates. This must be the only place in the world where the main road in and out crosses a runway.

We walked along Devils Tower Road, under the shadow of the sheer northern face of the rock. Looking upwards we could see high above us the holes in the rock face for the guns, which in the old days had made the rock impregnable. The hole led back into small rooms that had housed the guns. These rooms were all joined together by passages blasted and hewn out of the solid rock by the British Army between 1778 and 1783.

We visited these on one of our later walks and found them very interesting. All along the Galleries are glass cases holding life size models wearing the uniforms of the different Regiments? There are also tableaux depicting the soldiers manning the guns. Looking out from the gun rooms there are superb views overlooking the airport across the isthmus to Spain.

We walked on around to Catalan Bay, on our left the blue Mediterranean sea, and on our right the water catchment area which is formed of corrugated iron sheets laid side by side rising steeply halfway up the side-of the rock face and rears vertically to the top.

Catalan is a little fishing village clinging onto the base of the rock, its freshly painted multicolored houses, some with patios surrounded by bright red geraniums, make a picturesque splash, fronting the sea. It gives a Spanish flavour to the surroundings by the typical little church with flowers around the entrance. Fortunately, it also has a typically English pub in which we were glad to refresh ourselves with beer and a bar snack.

We continued on along the Sir Herbert Miles road passing Sandy Bay with some hotels arriving at a tunnel open only to traffic, pedestrians not being allowed. We were too tired by now to walk back, so holding hands we walked illegally for quite a distance through it, emerging into the open air overlooking the municipal rubbish dump.

The Lorries back up on a ramp to the edge of the cliff and tip the rubbish over, not a pretty sight but I expect it has improved by now.

A little further along was a clay pigeon shoot, the road then curves round to Europa Point. We had a good look round the light house, and the gun emplacement, taking the bus back into town .

I was awakened at 3 o'clock in the morning by Ron telling me not to panic but Blue Lizard was sinking! I quickly got dressed, went on deck, found Ron and asked the questions, "Are we still tied to her?" Yes! "Are we helping to keep her afloat?" Yes! "Will we sink with her?" Definitely not! "Good," I said, "I will make some tea."

Apparently, a plank had given way, the Fire Brigade was there pumping her out, hoping to keep the water at bay. Fortunately, they were successful making it possible to do a temporary repair by divers nailing a sheet of ply board over the damage.

Apparently, this was a common occurrence; the Fire Brigade spent more time pumping out boats than putting out fires. Everyone was glad of the tea it is always a good standby.

Sally was understandably close to tears, and needing lots of reassuring that her boat could and would be saved. Scotty and Ron were helping the fire brigade, though once the pumps were going there wasn't much any one could do, so I took Sally into our saloon until they were given the all clear to go back on the Blue Lizard.

Our preparations of Soñadora were going well we had made a permanent repair to the Black Duck. Trevor, after a great deal of difficulty with the Avon Company who was reluctant to either supply or tell him what adhesive was required, had managed to obtain and send us their special three part adhesive. The repaired seam gave us no further trouble all the way round the world.

One of our main problems now was our refrigeration system, which had been giving us trouble for some time. In the process of moving the engines forward in Santander we had to employ a local refrigeration expert to reposition the pipes from the compressor. Incredible as it might seem, the chap had tried to braze a rubber pipe, or at least the copper tag out of it, of course, ruining the entire pipe.

In the process of locating and obtaining a replacement, he had left the system open for such a long time that moisture had been allowed to enter. This moisture soon exhausted the dryers and would freeze in the expansion valves, stopping down the system. As we intended to refill the deep freeze with good British meat, cheese and butter, while in Gibraltar, it was essential that it was in good working order.

After much searching we managed to obtain the services of another refrigeration 'expert' who spent a day overhauling the system and replacing the dryers left after charging us a large sum of money, saying all our troubles were now over!

We had examined the bow damaged by the anchor, fortunately finding it was only superficial damage to the gel coat, which I replaced with difficulty standing in the repaired dinghy, as it bobbed up and down with the waves.

Some of the other yachts we had met were beginning to congregate here, ready for their trip to the Caribbean. Polack, Sylvia and also Simon, the chap who had come aboard in Bayona with his friend the inventor. Simon and his girlfriend came aboard one night and told us he had been in Gibraltar some time.

We had not seen his yacht because it was berthed around in the Marina behind the Water Port. He also had had his problems, shortly after his arrival in Gibraltar, he was walking back from the 'pens' along the causeway, when a car pulled up and the driver whom he had briefly met once before, offered him a lift into town. Simon was amazed when instead of stopping at the police gates at the end of road as signaled, the chap accelerated rapidly through! They were chased and soon stopped by a police car, Simon found himself in Jail!

The chap who had offered him the lift had stolen the car! Worse was to come, the chap didn't have any money and persuaded Simon to pay his bail for him. He then promptly disappeared which

Chapter 12 Gibraltar

left Simon very short of funds. To help himself out financially, he had taken on a paying passenger/crew, to cross the Atlantic with them. We didn't think this would work very well because it was quite a small yacht.

Gibraltar is a favourite place for crew to try and obtain a berth on a yacht. Many of them are experienced and good crew, but unfortunately the place also has lots of hippies, dropouts and addicts, the unfortunates of our modern society, many of them young girls. Most of them looking for a free trip to the Caribbean.

We and the other yachts were constantly pestered by them. This was brought home to us when we were there, by the wrecking of a very nice motor cruiser on the coast of Africa. A quite famous conjurer and magician travelled around living on his motor yacht and gave performances from place to place. His normal crew had had to leave him in Gibraltar.

He was unfortunate enough to take on one of these hippies to help keep watch on his way to the Canary Islands. When he was out of the Straits, he set the auto-pilot on the correct course, asked the crew to keep a good watch and to call him if there were any problems, and retired to get some sleep.

The next thing he knew they were aground on the hazardous African Coast, and they just managed to get ashore with their lives.

When he asked the crew what had happened, he was told, and that it was wrong that he should have such a beautiful boat. The chap had wrecked it deliberately! I would have killed him on the spot. Apparently, he just ran off.

The yacht owner went for help, but by the time he had managed to get back, the boat was a total wreck and everything salvageable had been stolen. As this was a deserted coastline it was suspected that this was a pre arranged job.

169

Having seen the problems that some unfortunate yacht owners who for some reason or other require crew, have to suffer, we are eternally thankful that we can manage easily on our own.

We had not yet visited the top of the rock, St. Michael's caves and the apes den, so we took the opportunity of another fine day to catch the cable car in the town and take the scenic ride to the top, a breath taking trip, with the whole town and harbour spread out beneath you.

A restaurant is incorporated into the top terminal of the cable lift; it was a really terrible place. A bare cheerless concrete building, with steel and plastic tables and chairs, and a poor cup of tea. We walked along the path at the very crest of the rock, looking down on the town on one side, the Mediterranean on the other. The terrain is wooded with stunted trees and thickly covered with bushes, giving off a heady smell; it was like walking through a pine forest at home. We explored the few disused and derelict observation posts and gun emplacements, and then walked on down the paths to St. Michaels caves.

We had the place to ourselves, the sun was shining, the birds were singing and there was an atmosphere of great calm and tranquility. It was delightful. We bought our tickets, and leaving the heat and glare of the sun behind us walked into another world. Cool and dimly lit, the sound of the beautiful base voice of the Russian singer, Ivan Rebroff came throbbing through the air. We stood spell bound, and looked and listened.

The main cave is very large, and during the Second World War was prepared as an emergency hospital, but was never used. It has since been turned into a theatre with seats rising in tiers from the stage, which is surrounded, by huge colorful stalactites and stalagmites. Some of which join to form large pillars creating a cathedral like atmosphere. The spotlights brought out the beautiful colours vividly, it was breath taking.

We sat in the auditorium and restfully listened to the music of Beethoven, Mozart and the singing of Rebroff, before looking around the rest of the caves which lead off from the main hall. This is 980 foot above sea level with countless other caves leading ever downwards, some still unexplored. There is a legend that there is a passage under the Straits to Africa from the bottommost caves, but it has never been discovered.

Many fossils of prehistoric animals, millions of years old, have been found in the caves and from the time of Neanderthal Man, man has taken refuge in them. We were very impressed and very sorry we had to leave Gibraltar without being able to attend a live concert there.

The Rock Apes in their Den

We continued on down to that part of the mountain side called the 'Apes Den' this is a popular place with the taxi drivers who take visitors on tours of the "Rock," there are always a few cabs or cars stopped there.

The apes roam freely about quite unconcerned about people, they vary in size from small cuddly babies who get themselves photographed sitting on peoples shoulders, to quite powerful creatures standing 3 to 4 ft high, who were not to be trifled with and can turn quite savage if teased. Ron was just advising me not to get too close to them, when it seemed as if one large male ape understood this, for he rushed over and promptly tore a side pocket off Ron's anorak, we couldn't help but laugh. The removal of the pocket had left a row of threads, which as we sat on a low wall, I started to remove. Ron pointed to a couple of apes delousing one another and laughingly said, "For goodness sake, stop, people will think you are delousing me!"

A little bit further on a baby ape was trying without success to pull the wing mirror off a car, as the occupants stood by taking photographs. The next moment a large ape rushed along the wall, and putting one hand on my head vaulted over me, leaping onto the car bonnet, and with one heave tore the wing mirror right off. It looked almost as if the little fellow had called for reinforcements. Very entertaining for everyone, but not the car owner, who drove off in a huff!

Leaving the apes behind we walked on down to the Moorish Castle, or rather what is left of it, for its walls once reached almost down to the sea. It is the Tower of Homage, which still looks very formidable, the bit that is left is still open to tourists but unfortunately on this day it was shut for repairs. The Castle has stood for twelve hundred years, and has withstood many sieges. At night when it is floodlit it can be seen from the town and from out in the Straits, and looks very impressive.

As we walked back along the pens, we were thankful to be called aboard Solaris Maiden for drinks, it had been an exhausting but enjoyable day. That evening we visited the Casino, not to gamble, but to have dinner and dance, Sally and Scotty joined us and we all had a very enjoyable time. This was a sort of farewell dinner to Gibraltar; we would be leaving in two days. It was late and we were very tired when we went to bed.

It seemed I had been asleep for only minutes when we

were awakened by crashes and shouting, as a yacht arrived. Ron went out into the cockpit just in time to see a crewman fall off the bow of the yacht, overreaching to catch a warp that had been thrown. Ron called me to come to watch the fun, and it was a few hectic moments before they got themselves sorted out. Meanwhile we had rescued the crewman who had been swimming in the filthy very cold and oily water. We took one look at him as he stood shivering on the deck, there was only one cure, a hot shower which he thankfully accepted, and called to his crew mates to bring some dry clothes. He departed with many thanks, carrying his bundle of wet togs with him. Only to return a few minutes later with an embarrassed look to present me with a pair of my panties which he had taken in error!

We had a busy day, loading the deep freeze, and taking on our final supply of stores. A tanker lorry arrived and we took on 250 gallons of diesel. We had managed to obtain a few second hand charts from various yachts, but had to go to the Naval Dock Yard Chart Office to buy the charts and pilots we still required. We had taken on 500 gallons of water, fortunately not water from the catchment, which was inclined to be rusty but straight from the desalination unit. All we had to come aboard now was our duty free spirits which were to be delivered in the morning just before we left. We intended to spend one day and night in Ceuta to take on fresh fruit and vegetables, wine, beer and gas which were all cheaper and better there.

This was our last night in Gibraltar, so we had a little farewell party on board, with our friends, many of whom wished they were joining us. Apparently Rilo had never seen Peter without his beard, and he joked that if he shaved it off he would be able to join us, as Rilo would never recognise him!

Malcolm had recently read an article in a yachting magazine reporting that 30 yachts had been lost without trace in the Caribbean that year, and we were regaled for quite a large part of the evening by tales of terror and destruction, attacks by whales and pirates, sinking and storms, even Ron's mother had managed to get into the act by sending us a letter with a newspaper cutting of a ship wreck, all in all an hilarious evening!

Monday the 15th of November dawned, it was a clear sunny morning, the Customs Officials arrived on time to seal the bonded stores, and by noon we were ready to depart. We had really enjoyed our time in Gibraltar, meeting many interesting people and making a few firm friends. I gave Malcolm my last letters to post, he cast off our warps and we all waved goodbye to each other as we motored slowly out into the harbour, their shouts of goodbye and happy sailing fading behind us. Again there was no wind, and we motored steadily across the straits taking our last look at the Rock as it receded into the haze.

My emotions were very mixed; I've always hated saying goodbye, for me it is the only real drawback to sailing around the world, where you are always heading on and not returning, I love the excitement of visiting new places, but unfortunately I hate saying goodbye to the old ones.

We tied up to Ceuta's concrete quay, astern of a large English yacht that had been just ahead of us all the way over. An official was waiting on the quay; we invited him aboard, and gave him a beer. He took our particulars, smiling when we said we had come from Malaga, accepted the few pesetas harbour dues for one night, and wished us "Buenos tardes".

We were soon ready and going ashore. As we passed the yacht in front, we heard the same official saying, "No, No, senor, you come from Malaga or Alicante, not possible Gibraltar" back came the firm reply "No, Gibraltar." Obviously nobody was going to tell this fellow where he had come from! We saw the official throw up his hands as we continued on into town.

We had been told that the islands in the Caribbean liked to

see a yachts clearance papers from the previous port and we spent a couple of fruitless hours trying to get one, going from one office to another, but in the end we had to be satisfied with a stamp in our passports, and even that took a lot of getting.

On our way back to Soñadora we called in at the supermarket close to the dock. We borrowed two large trolleys from them and loaded them with cases of wine, beer, Cointreau and other Spanish liquors, which were very cheap here then. A case of Skol beer 24 bottles was £1.50! In the Caribbean then 1 bottle could cost 50p!! As we were pushing our trolleys past the British yacht, there were several officials on board, and everything was out on the quay, they were being thoroughly searched. We felt very sorry for both parties, the officials certainly hadn't wanted to do it, but that was the rule for any yacht coming from Gibraltar and the British chap had left them no choice.

We were walking back from returning the trolleys when to our surprise we saw 'Solaris' coming in across the harbour. We were just in time to take his warps astern of us. Malcolm had decided that, as it was such a nice day to come over for gas and take us to dinner, what a lovely surprise. That evening Malcolm took us to his favourite little Spanish restaurant, after a good meal with good wine, we walked slowly back through the town enjoying the cool of the night. We had coffee and liquors on Soñadora and retired early after arranging that in the morning Ron and Malcolm would go for the gas while I went to get the fresh fruit and vegetables from the market.

By noon the following day we had all completed our missions and we were ready to sail. Everything had been checked, the sails were already hanked on, and for the first time in weeks a Levanter was blowing, out of the straights just what we wanted, and what tide there was, was with us. Ron started the engines and you could almost feel Soñadora come to life, saying, "Come on we have a good wind and tide, let's go." Malcolm cast off our warps and for the last time we waved goodbye to him, moving away towards the harbour entrance, keeping a good look out for our old enemy the 'Algeciras' ferry, hoisting the mainsail as we went. What ever happened now we were on our way, for the first time we were going to be hundreds of miles off land and any troubles we had coming we were going to have to face totally on our own.

Once into the straits of Gibraltar the autopilot was set heading due south. The engines were left ticking over in case of emergencies while we had our first try at goose winging the sails. The main was already up just needing a preventer which Ron attached from the end of the boom to a cleat on the bow deck port side.

Next we attached the 22ft whisker pole to the mast by lifting one end up and clipping it into a socket that slides on a track up the lower part of the mast. The other end is supported by a topping lift from high up the mast and is prevented fore and aft by guy ropes taken to the bow and stern. The sheet from the Genoa is led through a claw at the end of the pole holding the sail out wide from the mast goosed winged to starboard to match the Main sail which is goose winged to the port side. This brings the wind behind both sails which is the best point of sailing for a cat. But this needs to be constantly monitored and easy to release if there was a sudden change of course or wind direction.

Ron winched the No 1 Genoa up the forestay while   I started to wind in the sheet on our big cockpit winch. We now had 1,600 sq. foot of sail set. Soñadora looked like a big white bird with its wings spread wide rushing comfortably along. It was very exciting!

Goose Wing Rig

To goose wing the sails on Soñadora had taken us about half an hour. During this time the wind speed had increased to about 35 knots and our speed on the log was surging from 15 to well over 20 knots. As we were running away from the wind all we could feel of this gale was a nice breeze, cold enough for a sweater, but very exhilarating.

Soñadora ploughed her way out into the Atlantic making twin white wakes combining in the middle to form one high foaming rooster tail behind her. Watching it was hypnotic.

Rising to the top of wave

Going down the crest of wave, a very smooth motion

We had never had Soñadora so heavily laden. The last time she had achieved these speeds had been on the trip from Dartmouth to Southampton when she had weighed less than 10 tons. Now we were nearly 20 tons and it didn't seem to affect her at all. She was surfing down the waves with not a care in the world enjoying every minute of it and so were we. After our hectic efforts getting her sails rigged we decided we had earned a drink. We had a beer each not forgetting to wet Soñadora decks to include her in the celebrations. We also splashed a little overboard as a libation to Neptune.

We sat on the cabin top on the port side drinking our beer and watching the coastline of North Africa wiz by. We were very pleased to be leaving the Straits getting out into the Atlantic in this easy fashion.

Because of the recent vagaries of the weather we had thought it highly possible we would have to motor out straight into the teeth of a head wind. One yacht somewhat lacking in power had left Gibraltar and spent 2 days trying to beat out before giving up and returning.

As we watched the Bay of Tangier with its town spreading back over the hills quickly disappear, we realised at long last we were on our way. I was feeling so happy and excited. I leaned over, hugged and kissed Ron. He must have been feeling the same for we just sat there for a long time with our arms around each other too contented to move.

On the northwest extremity of Africa is a very distinctive black, hammock shaped rock rising 1,000 feet high. This was the last bit of land we would see until we reached the Canaries providing Ron's untried astronavigation worked.

By the time it was dark we were more than 25 miles straight out to sea and at last out of range of the Cabot Esparto lights. It was to be four years before we were to see its light again.

The coast of Africa is quite treacherous with in-shore currents and we had decided to stand well out to sea before turning southwest for the Canaries. Our course change would take place in the early morning. If the wind was still in the same direction the running pole would have to be taken down requiring the two of us. As I was feeling quite tired, Ron said he would take the first watch from 20:00 to 24:00 hours. After an excellent dinner of steak and chipped potatoes I said goodnight to Ron, put on my nightie and thankfully climbed into my bunk leaving Ron taking his ease in the cockpit sipping a gin and tonic!

I lay in my bunk listening to the waters swish by with an occasional loud thump as the odd wave hit the side of the hull. We were now well out into the Atlantic. Strong winds had built up a large sea, but being goose winged the motion of Soñadora was very pleasant. I hardly had time to go over the events of the day before I was fast asleep.

My pleasant dreams were rudely interrupted by both engines roaring into life followed by a loud crash-bang as the sails went aback and Soñadora started a short quick roll. She came beam-on to the big seas. I was out into the cockpit before Ron could shout to me. It was pitch dark and Ron was at the wheel. Just ahead of us to starboard I could see the stern of a medium sized cargo ship its decks and bridge brightly lit. Ron was cursing flashes. I asked what had happened. He said, "I'll tell you later. Let's get this 'B' mess sorted out first."

We had never been confronted with anything like this before. We had been running before the wind which meant that the speed of the boat was in effect deducted from the speed of the wind. So if the boat was doing 15 knots and the wind speed was 30 knots the effective load on the sails and rigging was only approximately 15 knots and our 1,600 sq ft. of sail had been quite reasonable. Now that we were beam onto the wind the pressure on the rigging and sails was the full 30 knots or more. I didn't have a chance to look at the wind speed instrument to find out. I only knew it was blowing like hell and I was very cold in my nightie!!

We were now in the difficult position of having the Genoa aback meaning the wind on the front of it was putting all the strain on the whisker pole and front guy and the wind on the correct side of the main one cancelling out the other. Ron had started the engines in the hope he could turn Soñadora to run before the wind again but he had no chance. The pressure on the sails was tremendous. The only thing to do was to get rid of the 1,000 sq ft. Genoa. We had never had to drop it when it was aback before and had no idea how it would come down. We still had our safety lines rigged and wore our safety harnesses to work on deck in rough weather. Because we were afraid that we might lose the mast I didn't waste time putting more clothes on, I just put on the harness and battled my way down the heaving deck to help get the sail under control. Ron went to the foot of the mast to release the halyard. When he did so the sail came down a little way and stopped. Ron fought his way down to the fore stay hampered by his harness and life lines, but managed to heave it down the rest of the way while I leapt around like a demented flea trying to smother the sail to stop the wind blowing it overboard. Ron joined me and we eventually managed to get it stowed in a forward sail locker.

Panic was over for a while. We unraveled ourselves and our lifelines making our way back to the cockpit. I began to feel the cold for the first time. I went below for some warm clothes. I made a hot cup of Bovril each while Ron got Soñadora back on course. This had taken over half an hour and the ship that had caused the trouble had long since disappeared. We sat in the cockpit drinking our Bovril as Ron told me what had happened.

About an hour before I had been awakened so abruptly Ron had seen the lights of a ship appear over the horizon behind us. All had seemed well for a while when he noticed the red and green navigation lights of the ship indicating it was coming up dead astern. Ron changed course to port as much as he could, but was amazed to see the ship alter course to match. He then altered course to starboard whereupon the ship did the same. He changed course several more times like this, but each time the ship followed until after about an hour it was so close astern that Ron could light it up with our powerful search light. There was no doubt that the ship could see us and was deliberately following our course. By this time we were lit up like a Christmas tree with every possible light on. It was now so close that Ron did the only thing left to do start the engines and at the eleventh hour turn hard to port. The ship passed much too close to our starboard side. It went by missing our stern by feet! Ron played the searchlight on the bridge and could see several men looking at us.

This was a very frightening experience. One we fortunately have never had since. We could only guess that they had been intrigued to know what small vessel was making such good speed and had come close to investigate. They obviously had no idea of the problems a ship presents to a yacht at close quarters in the open sea. All in all it was an example of extremely poor seamanship on their part.

By the time we had finished our drink the wind had started to drop and within half an hour had disappeared altogether. We checked our log and found that Soñadora had travelled 140 miles in 10 hours an average speed of 14 knots.

To be becalmed after a blow is a most uncomfortable experience. It was more than we felt like putting up with on this night. We dropped and secured the 'main' now that the wind had gone away and we switched to one engine to keep us moving. Ron went off watch. I kept watch and the autopilot did the steering.

Our watch keeping consists of a good look all around the horizon at 10-minute intervals or less if required. If a ship gets close enough for us to see their navigation lights we keep a constant watch until they have passed.

We found over the years that many of the ships that pass by day and night are on autopilot with no watch keeping at all. We have trained our searchlight on them and signaled without reply. When I am not looking around the horizon I have a lovely time reading, playing patience or scrabble, writing letters etc., or watching the stars and trying to identify them.

Some nights when the moon is full it is just beautiful to lie in the cockpit and watch the changing shapes of the clouds as they glide over the face of the moon. It always fascinates me how the silver pathway that the moonlight makes across the sea always comes directly toward us. People often ask me do I get bored on night watch, but I rarely do as there is so much to look at when you have the time to really stop and look.

There is one hard and fast rule that the person on watch has to obey. Never leave the cockpit to go on deck without waking the other. This way the one off watch can relax knowing that the other won't have disappeared overboard without their knowing. When a yacht is on autopilot there is a real danger that someone may have gone overboard and you wouldn't know immediately. Trust is paramount to peace of mind. By 04:00 hours I felt so sleepy that I just had to wake Ron up. This is another one of our safety rules; getting over tired at sea is perhaps the biggest killer of all. This time my sleep was undisturbed. Ron had let me sleep on. It was 10 am when I eventually awoke very refreshed having had a full six hours sleep. There had been enough wind to sail for some time. As he would have had to wake me before leaving the cockpit to get the sails up he had decided to motor on and let me sleep. After we had set the sails and stopped the engine I went below to make breakfast.

We were both starving so it was bacon, eggs and plenty of toast. It was a very pleasant morning. The seas had gone down, the sun was shining brightly and we had a little over 10 knots of cool wind. Soñadora was slipping quietly through the water between 5 - 6 knots. We were totally alone on an empty expanse of sea with just the occasional sea bird.

Later as we sat on deck we discussed the events of the night. We were pretty satisfied with how we had coped with the emergency and were again reassured by the strength of Soñadora. Once again, thank goodness, she had proved herself almost idiot proof. We were the right ones to test her as it seemed we could only learn by experience!

184

One thing we had learned that night was never to run using a boomed out mainsail. We now realised what a difficult sail the main was to get rid of quickly. To drop it one has to bring the yacht's head into the wind to relieve the pressure on the slides in the mast track. This can be a difficult and dangerous task in a gale with a big sea running. When running down wind we now always rig two whisker poles and use two Genoas. Using our largest Genoas we can set 2,200 square feet of sail and get rid of it easily while still running in a matter of minutes.

Ron started to put his astronavigation into practice for the first time as opposed to theory with not a great deal of success. His position seemed to place us somewhere in the middle of the Sahara Desert. We had a good laugh deciding as we had enough stores and water on board for a year we could afford one small mistake. Big navigational errors like this are so gross they are obvious. It is the small plausible ones that are dangerous.

Ron just checked that there was sea around us and not sand, and worked his figures again. Finding we were at sea and somewhere near where we should be (we hoped) the rest of the day passed pleasantly uneventful.

That night I took the first watch. Fortunately for cruising purposes Ron can drop off to sleep at any time and prefers to go to sleep early. On land this annoys me no end as I am reaching my best at midnight and like to go to sleep late. I remember in Santander some Spanish friends took us on a tour of the local night clubs. To their amazement as soon as Ron sat down he fell fast asleep. We had to wake him up each time we moved to another club. When asked the next morning how he had enjoyed himself he replied, "it was the most expensive sleep he had ever had!"

At sea this works very well. We find that the traditional two/four hour watches don't work for us as we don't have to man the wheel. We find that longer watches are not so tiring. I usually take the 20:00 to 02:00 watch and sometimes if I am not tired I let Ron sleep longer. Ron then takes over the watch leaving me to sleep if there is nothing to do until I wake up naturally. This means we always get six hours and sometimes eight hours uninterrupted sleep. This is very important at sea. Some people do not realise that the body muscles are constantly countering the motion of the boat and this is very tiring. That night I woke Ron at 03:00 with a cup of cocoa. I reported no alarms, no ships and that we were still sailing, but very slowly. I took myself to bed.

When I woke the sun was shining brightly, the wind had almost disappeared and we were barely moving. I stripped off to get an allover tan and tried to persuade Ron to do the same, but without success. He claims there are too many hazards lurking aboard a yacht to go galloping about with all one's crown jewels exposed to snaggings in the rigging etc! With a twinkle in my eye I told him it's such a little thing to make such a fuss about!!

Ron managed to get a good noon sight, navigation it seems is mostly a question of confidence. Ron was getting more used to handling the sextant. He couldn't have had a better time to practice because the sea was quite calm and there was hardly any movement on Soñadora.

Shortly after the noon sighting the wind dropped completely. It was time to start an engine. The engines have to be run once in every 24 hours for 1 to 2 hours to maintain the fridge/freezer. It also heats our hot water and charges our batteries for the lighting, autopilot, pumps etc. We try to fit this in as far as possible with periods of no wind, killing two birds with one stone.

Ron decided to check the oil and water and grease the stem glands. While he was in the engine room a cheeky little bird came aboard. It flew into the engine room and buzzed Ron's head giving him quite a fright. Not the sort of thing you expect on a well run boat! It flew out of the engine room and straight into the saloon. It was quite tame but wouldn't accept any food or water. It seemed to want a rest so we encouraged him to settle in among the books.

In the afternoon we spread the long cockpit seats on the cabin top. We had long since dropped the sails which with no wind slat around making a dreadful noise. They do themselves more damage doing this than when we are sailing hard. We lay there on our deck mattresses reading and listening to the radio with an occasional scotch or gin and tonic to settle the digestion. We had a good look round the horizon from time to time. A very difficult job this cruising - really takes it out of you!!

These conditions continued for the next few days. We alternated between sailing and motoring though we could have done with a little more constant wind. We couldn't have wished for a more pleasant introduction to our first ocean crossing. We had been at sea a week when Ron woke me up with a cup of tea and said, "Carole wake up here is your tea, bring it out on deck we have visitors." Of course, it was the dolphins and this is where we came in.

I can only repeat what I said in the introduction. They really are the most happy and endearing of all the creatures we meet at sea. You feel happier just seeing them.

Another thing that endears them to Ron is that they seem to like Mozart and Beethoven. We always put a tape on for them and turn the volume up. We often see them looking up at us. Listening to their high pitched squeaks we wonder if they are discussing what we look like. It would be interesting and fun to know what they think of us.

That evening I was sitting in the cockpit watching the sun going down when I saw a most peculiar sight in the sky on the horizon ahead of us. It was a huge grayish white mushroom shaped cloud. It looked exactly like photographs I had seen of an atomic explosion. I felt quite cold! I called Ron out to see it and he decided after a while that the people in the Canaries must have heard we were coming and decided to self-destruct! It made me laugh, but I still felt quite spooked. It was still there when the sun went down.

The next day Ron had taken his sun sights as normal, but idle as ever he only just got around to doing the mathematics late in the afternoon. We were sitting in the saloon and Ron looked up and said, "if my calculations are correct you should see the island of Tenerife out the starboard window." I thought he was pulling my leg. I looked out the window straight into the setting sun. I was just saying, "I can't see anything," when the sun went behind a huge mountain. We rushed into the cockpit for a better view and to make sure our eyes were not deceiving us. It was really there. The very distinctive cone shaped top of the Pico Mountain is an impressive first sight of land after eight days at sea.

"This navigation stuff must really work," said Ron. Up until this moment I don't think he had really believed in it. He was as pleased as punch and so was I. We have since made hundreds of landfalls, but nothing compares with the first time, just like being in love! I went in and fetched out a bottle of Spanish wine. It was a wonderful moment and we sat there happily toasting ourselves and Soñadora. It suddenly occurred to us that at our present speed we would arrive at our destination, which was the Island of Gran Canarias, in the dark which we didn't want to do. We slowed right down. First light found us off the port of Las Palmas.

We had not originally intended to come to Gran Canarias. We had heard the port was very dirty and oily, but we had no option as the agents for our sailing instruments were based there. They were supposed to be supplying spares and repairing our instruments which had given trouble since they were first fitted.

We motored into Puerto de la Luz and headed toward where we could see a few yachts. I looked down into a black sea of oil - all the stories we had heard were true and our hearts sank. Poor Soñadora. What a mess she was going to get into. What were we to do? Any dinghy or warps put into this black oil slick would be ruined. We had just not been able to visualize how bad it would be. Even here on the outer fringe of the harbour it looked to be six feet deep in oil. We were just about to abandon the idea and head down to the southern end of the island where we had heard there was a new marina when a man appeared on a yacht that was tied to an old fishing boat alongside the quay. He waved inviting us to tie alongside him.

Once we had checked that our warps and spring lines were not going to touch the water, we accepted his kind invitation to come aboard for coffee. He was an American named Bon in his 60's and reminded us very much of Bing Crosby in looks and mannerisms. I quite expected him to burst into song at any moment! His yacht was an exact replica of Slocomb's famous yacht Spray. He had built it 20 years previously in Nova Scotia almost in the same field where Slocomb had rebuilt Spray. Bob had built everything himself even to felling the trees for timber for the hull and masts etc. and had forged all the metal work in his own forge.

It had canvas sails, hemp warps and tarred rigging. The interior gave the impression of a combination of log cabin and an old sailing ship. There was a wood burning stove by the mast base where he did all his cooking. Logs for the stove were stored in the fo'c'sle. His dry stores were stowed in large galvanised dustbins. He did not have an engine not even an outboard. We were fascinated. It was like stepping back into history. The smell of tarred ropes, burning logs, pipe tobacco and freshly baked bread took us back into another age.

We listened to Bob's quiet drawl as he told us about the building of his boat and the years when he had first used her to carry gravel up the Hudson River. He decided that the years were whizzing by and that if he was going to sail and see a bit of the world in her he had better get going. He had taken the northern route across the Atlantic and then turned south to the Azores's and onto The Canaries. He had enjoyed his trip. Had no problems from icebergs, but had encountered an even stranger obstacle in those waters. Bob's soft American drawl and quiet unassuming manner added comedy to his story as he told us, "I was down below decks making my breakfast after a rough night when I felt a bump as something hit me. I went above to see what it was. I could hardly believe my eyes. There was one of these little plastic type yachts with its bowsprit caught up in my rigging." A man appeared and while untangling his yacht he told me that he was taking part in the Single Handed Trans-Atlantic Race and had been taking some sleep when we collided. I offered him some breakfast, but he wouldn't stop. He was in such a hurry to be off again, that it only seemed minutes before he disappeared. I began to wonder if it had really happened. Such a pity he didn't stay and enjoy the moment of a life time. It will never happen again. Anyway, he was lucky I hadn't damaged him.

By now it was 10:30 am and we thought we had better make our arrival official. We thanked Bob for his hospitality and stepped ashore. Near the end of the quay was a little shed where the harbour official or policeman or whatever his official status was, was lurking. He took one look at us and disappeared into the distance at great speed. We never did manage to meet him and failed to find any way to enter or clear officially other than reporting in at the yacht club. We then went to the post office, but we had no mail. If any mail had been sent to the Canaries we never received it.

After much searching we managed to locate the agent for our instruments, discovering that they knew less about them than we did. They had no spares, no wiring diagrams and the firm in England had not contacted them as they had promised they would do. So our visit to the oily port was in vain.

We were walking back to Soñadora feeling very despondent with the oily harbour on one side and the dirty port town on the other. Ron was complaining bitterly saying he couldn't understand how thousands of people came here for a holiday. I suggested we should find a bar and cheer ourselves up. We turned right into a street we thought would lead us to the centre of town. After a few hundred yards, to our amazement, we emerged into a different world. There was a promenade facing a beach of golden sand crowded with happy sun-tanned holiday makers mostly German and Scandinavian. We had crossed the island from East to West. In those few hundred yards the contrast was incredible. We went into a bar and some wag had put up a sign saying 'Spanish spoken here.'

Feeling much more cheerful we were walking back along the dock to Soñadora when Ron said, "Look! Doesn't that red fez look familiar to you? It's that chap we saw rowing his little yacht out of Gibraltar." It certainly looked like him only this time he was paddling along in a little inflatable plastic canoe with Indian chiefs' head painted on its bow! He looked just as comical as he had the first time we saw him in Gibraltar. As we watched he reached the back of Bob's boat and went aboard. We arrived a few moments later and Bob introduced us to him. He still had his fez on but it turned out to be the leg of a pair of trousers! He was German, but unfortunately I can't remember his name. We invited him and Bob aboard for a drink.

As we relaxed in the cockpit enjoying one of the favourite occupations of yachtsmen (exchanging yarns) we were surprised to learn that the little yacht we thought would have trouble crossing the Straits of Gibraltar let alone cross to the Caribbean, had in fact brought him safely here. It was quite a sad and amazing story he told us.

He had first sailed to the Caribbean with his wife in a 50 ft yacht some years before. Both enjoyed it very much. On returning to Germany they had decided to repeat the voyage again the following season. In order to finance this he had sold his 50 ft yacht and bought a 45 ft one. Again both enjoyed the trip. This went on year after year with the yachts getting smaller and smaller until this year it was so small that his wife refused to come with him.

However the sea had got such a firm grip of him that he had decided to come on his own. Sadly his wife divorced him. This obviously had upset him very much because he never stopped talking about her and their adventures together.

Bob was telling him about his collision with the yacht in the North Atlantic and he went on to tell us about an experience he and his wife had had in the Caribbean.

They were becalmed in an empty ocean and had gone below to catch up with their lovemaking. Time obviously must have flown for them because they were roused out of their euphoria by a sudden violent motion of the yacht. Dashing on deck in the nude they were astounded to see a large liner heaved to alongside them. There were hundreds of people lining the rails clicking away with their cameras and gazing down at them in wonder! It was such a sad tail I wanted to give him a hug, but thought he might not like a comparatively new acquaintance attacking him.

The following morning we awoke to the tantalizing aroma of freshly baking bread. As soon as I emerged on deck Bob handed me a hot wholemeal loaf fresh from the oven. We had it with breakfast. It was delicious. What a contrast to my efforts. I am told I am quite a good cook, but I just can't seem to make bread. I have had many people show me different ways of baking it. I am always successful when they are with me, but have disastrous results on my own. On one occasion after practicing at home the loaves turned out so heavy that I gave them to Pat for her chickens. She had to soak them before they could eat them.

We had a pleasant morning exploring the town and came back laden with fresh fruit and vegetables. We told Bob we would be leaving the following morning early for Puerto Rico at the southern end of the island and invited him to dinner that night. Bob intended to head for the Caribbean but wasn't sure where. He had a chart of Barbados but no courtesy flag. He had heard that the officials got very uptight if you didn't fly the Barbados flag. He had been unable to obtain one here and was a bit worried about it. We sat together and I made one from a piece of his old blue denims and some scraps of material that I had.

Early next morning we cast off from alongside Bob, taking care that no warps dropped in the oil and motored slowly out of the harbour waving goodbye to Bob as we went. We hoped that we would meet up again sometime but we never did. We often wondered where he was.

We had a good wind and brisk sail down to Puerto Rico which turned out to be a new manmade harbour solely for yachts. This was part of a large German financed holiday complex. We found a nice long easy quay to tie to just inside of the entrance to the harbour. We were pleased to see the waters were beautifully clean.

For once in Spain officialdom was very prompt. We scarcely had time to secure our warps when two of them appeared and asked how long were we staying, wrote us out a bill for two nights and told us it was payable at once.

We made sure Soñadora was comfortable at her moorings and took a walk along the quay looking at the yachts. We were told nearly 211 of them, mostly foreign, were getting ready for their trip across to the Caribbean. At the far end we were pleased to see a yacht we knew. It was Simon and Elaine who you may remember had left Gibraltar with their Chinese Canadian crew. We were welcomed aboard and handed a beer. I noticed Simon didn't look or sound too well. They had had a rough trip. Simon had become ill, they suspected from some kind of poison. When they arrived he had gone to the hospital. They gave him a course of antibiotics and an anti-tetanus injection to which he reacted quite severely. He was only just beginning to recover and was feeling quite depressed when we saw him. It was as we had feared. The new crew person he had taken on in Gibraltar, although a pleasant chap had been quite useless. To add to this Simon's engine had seized up and was now in little pieces on the quay. It was beyond repair and he was hoping to sell it for spares.

Later that evening they all came aboard Soñadora   for a drink bringing with them Glyn another single hander also bound for the Caribbean. He had sailed direct from England and was telling us about an odd sight he had seen just off Tenerife. As he started to speak I knew exactly what he was going to say it was our atomic mushroom cloud. He was very relieved when I told him we had seen it too. He had been afraid that in being on his own for so long he was beginning to see things. We enjoyed the evening very much.

The next day we explored the nearest village which had been built entirely from scratch as part of the German project. They had made quite a good job of it. The flats had been built into the hills overlooking the harbour. They were well laid out gardens, tennis courts, squash courts, bowling alleys etc., and a small shopping centre which I found very expensive. For the last few items I wanted for our trip I took a bus to the nearest old village ten miles away. The surrounding country was very dry and arid, but the little village was very pleasant and my shopping cost me half as much.

It was now Tuesday 30th November 1976 and time to be on our way for Antigua in the Caribbean if we wanted to be there for Christmas. I cleaned the inside of the boat while Ron borrowed Simon's dinghy to scrub off the hulls underwater with a long handled brush as he didn't fancy diving in the cold water. We filled our water tanks. Ron checked the engines and we had our lunch deciding we were as ready as we ever would be. We cast off from the quay, waved goodbye to Simon and set sail for our first major ocean crossing of approximately 2,500nm Miles.

O n leaving the shelter of the Island we met 15 knots of wind and a short choppy sea. We left the port engine running to charge the batteries, hoisted the No.1 Genoa, set the autopilot on course bound for Antigua, in the Caribbean and settled down in the cockpit for a celebration drink, not forgetting Soñadora and Neptune as we took our last look at land for about three weeks.

Conditions were beginning to get worse and we noticed a yacht that had left before us heading back to port, may be they had just gone out for a quick sail??? It was dark at 18.00 hours, by which time we had the sails, Main and Genoa set for the night, we had settled down well feeling quite in tune with being at sea again.

After dinner we decided to split the night watch into three, from 20.00 hrs, to 24.00 hrs 24 to 04.00 and 04.00 to 08.00 hrs, Ron taking the first watch, I wasn't able to sleep, feeling just a little sea sick, the first time since the Bay of Biscay, so I settled down on the saloon seat, which lays athwart ships, so is the most comfortable area in a rough sea. By the time Ron came to relieve me the wind had veered to N.E. rising to 30 knts. It was time to change down sails to a working jib Ron had no trouble getting to sleep after that activity.

Wednesday December 1st 1976. The early hours of the morning brought no improvement in the weather, but it never seems so bad when dawn is breaking, Ron decided we should put up a larger sail, so we poled out a No.1 with an instant improvement in our speed. We had a lazy snooze morning, it was surprisingly cold so we shut the cabin door and kept watch from the comfort of the saloon, and fortunately the cabin windows afford a good all-round view.

Ron's noon sight though difficult to get, a combination of cloud, and a moving deck, put us heading in the right direction so with that burst of energy we settled down again to rest.

Rest! The gods must have been listening and thought we needed a sharp reminder that we were at sea, there was such a sudden deterioration in the weather that a quick change down to storm jib was required. Ron said he could manage, but being a willing little worker I insisted in helping him, and pulled the release cord on the whisker pole just as Ron was reaching up to catch it as he lowered it down. Relieved of the weight of its sail the pole sprang into life, bounced on my head and gave Ron a glancing blow on his shoulder as it crashed to the deck.

I saw stars and sat down, I couldn't help but laugh though, Ron wasn't at all amused, and I was rudely told to get back to the cockpit before I got us both killed. With the storm jib set, Genoa and pole stowed Ron returned to the saloon rubbing his shoulder, looking worried "My god Carole that was a close shave, do you realise what could have happened?" "What do you mean we only had a couple of bruises, nothing to shout about?" I replied." "Carole that pole could have knocked us both overboard and with Soñadora on autopilot, that would have been the end of us. From now on even in daylight, if the weather is rough and we have to go up forward we wear our safety belts, clipped onto the deck safety lines I don't want any arguments, that's it." I could tell he was cross, I am quick! So I agreed reluctantly, Ron knew I didn't like wearing it, but I could see his point. I must admit it was a horrible picture he had painted; I could just see us both there in the sea splashing about shouting "Hey Soñadora wait for us!"

This sharp reminder of the dangers of being knocked overboard in rough weather prompted us the following day to discuss rescue plans, which should have happened before we left the UK though we did have a very substantial first aid kit, and a defibrillator.

We listed all the different situations we could think of. Day/Night. Male/Female. - Injuries, - Conscious - unconscious. - Equipment to hand. Number of people on board taking into accounts the differences in their weight, height and strengths, this is what we came up with, for two people.

1.   Quickly shout MAN OVER BOARD even when there are only two of you, it helps to focus the mind and reassures the person in the water that you have the situation in hand. While shouting, throw the life ring in, which should have a flashing light and whistle attached, also the Dan Buoy (a 10ft Pole with a float at one end, and a red marker flag at the other) overboard to the person.

2.   Drop the sails, start both engines and turn Soñadora round on a reciprocal course on the auto pilot.

3.   Get 3 warps tie two with loops at one end, for the person in the water to put their feet into, to help them get up the ladder, secure the other two ends to a cleat, on deck, tie the 3rd warp to yourself and the other end to a cleat, again on deck, If possible lower the boarding ladder

4.   On reaching the person (probably Ron being knocked over by helpful Carole) put the engines in neutral before throwing the warps over the side so they don't get caught in the propellers, making doubly sure the other ends are tied to cleats.

5.   Unless the person is in great difficulty or the person is unconscious, never get into the sea to help, stay on board to instruct the person to put their feet into the loops of the warps or under their arms, get them to the ladder and winch them in.

6.   If one has to go in, make sure you are firmly tied to the boat. (You may laugh but on numerous occasions I have been handed a

warp by the owner to make his yacht fast to Soñadora only to discover he has forgotten to secure the other end to his own boat).

7.   If the person is secured to the yacht by the warps, but hasn't the strength to climb aboard, swing the boom out and try to hoist him up and in, or as a last resort lower the dinghy and get the person into it to recover his strength to help himself to get back on board, or put a warp on a winch the other end looped under his arms. To winch him in.

8.   If it is night time we have a very powerful halogen search light which penetrates the water giving clearer visibility. As opposed to any other type of light which only reflects on the surface of the water. Switch all the ships lights on.

9.   Rescue at sea can be a very tricky situation, if it is dark, it is almost impossible. All trips are different and every trip should be planned for, as if it was your first.

*****

        The rough weather seemed set for the night, but with the storm jib already up, Ron felt confident he wouldn't need to change sails again until day light, so we divided the night into two, me to take the first watch, so Ron could have a really good night's sleep, but we would leave our safety harnesses on for the rest of the night

        The main advantage of wearing a safety line is that it leaves both hands free to work with, usually without a safety line; it is one hand for yourself holding on, and the other to work with, which can be a bit tiresome.

        It was still pretty rough and cold, so I went into the warm saloon, Ron following. It wasn't until I went to take off my harness that I suddenly realised that I hadn't actually unclipped it from the forward pulpit, and theoretically, I should still be out there. I had a job persuading Ron that I hadn't unclipped it. It had unclipped itself during my frantic activity, goodness knows when, but it gave me a cold feeling to think I had been relying on my belt for safety and not my hands. We examined the belt and discovered that it could quite easily be unclipped, it only had to twist on itself and that was it.

So only one day after agreeing to wear it in rough weather, Ron was agreeing it was better to rely on yourself than a belt that gave a false sense of security. Our belts were the clip on types, and we have only worn them at night and in very bad weather since, but still keeping a hand for our selves, I am sure they have been improved since 1975.

Even with the big sea's we were soon sailing along at a steady 7 knots. At long last the sun had come out. Unfortunately, for me also out came the sextant; Ron had decided it was time for me to learn how to navigate.

While I agree it is always a good idea to know approximately where you are heading, my eyes did not, they were having trouble adjusting to reading print in motion, while looking through the sextant at a very wavy horizon, to bring a reluctant sun down to meet it, balancing on a moving deck, with a stomach that is not quite sure it belongs to you. It is a bit like trying to study the stars while sitting on a rocking horse. I quickly gave up trying, there is always to-morrow, (thank goodness for the GPS of today). I studied the theory instead, made easy with Ron's formula and took on the task of timing the sights while Ron using the sextant, took them. 3 before noon and 3 after, taking the mean average gives a very accurate time. I can now find land if I have too, but I will never be as good as Ron was with a sextant. He has never been more than 4 miles off course even after 35 days at sea with land fall being a tiny Pacific Island with the highest thing on it being a palm tree.

Friday 3rd December 1976. The next ten days were a mixture of bright sunny spells, variable winds, squall's, calms, and not very warm, but we were thoroughly enjoying it. My feeling of sea sickness had gone, we had been getting plenty of sleep, which meant that during the day, my thoughts naturally turned to food, as soon as we had, had one meal, I was planning the next. Poor Ron didn't stand a chance, and it wasn't until we were given a picture of ourselves in Antigua that we realised just how fat we were. It was quite a shock. We are the only two I know who put on weight at sea! I blamed the deep freezer, and Soñadora's stability, Ron just blames me. But there is nothing to beat sitting in the cockpit, in the middle of an Ocean, in complete isolation with the one you love watching the sun go down with a glass of wine followed by a good roast dinner. It is just perfect!

Carole and Ron in Antigua January 1977

We were now into the routine of dividing the night into two, Ron going to sleep first 20-00 hrs, until 13-00/14-00 hrs. Depending how tired I was, then Ron takes over and waking me any time after 08-00 hrs. We found that this was the best for us, we seldom got really tired, and it leaves the day time free to enjoy it together, and I can spend my night watch, doing the once daily washing up, cleaning where required, do my writing, reading, playing cards, scrabble and listening to music, while keeping a good look out. It is very pleasant and the time just flies by. Ron does the general maintenance, chart work, navigation, reads and likes his music, he even goes to sleep with his radio plugged into his ear, strange! I keep telling him he is not giving his brain time to relax and unscramble itself, his reply was "What brain??"

We were making good progress averaging 5-6-7 knots, giving 128/157 nautical miles in 24 hours. It was still fairly cold at night with not much sea life, only a few Storm Petrels. Regardless of the seastate they are so good to watch flying and skimming the top of the waves, with not a care in the world.

We had started to clean up the white paint work on Soñadora's topsides while at the same time I was trying to get an all over tan. I could not persuade Ron to strip off. He said he was not risking getting his "crown jewels" caught up in the rigging, Shame! However, I need not to have bothered as the sun didn't last for long.

Ten days had gone by during which we had had lots of rain squalls with winds gusting from 35 to 40 knts. This required Ron to man the wheel as the autopilot could not take the sudden changes of wind speeds with the sails up.

We had just had the first good night's sleep in three days, the weather was still rough. Where oh where are the so called trade winds? When daylight came Ron discovered that the wind had blown the end of the starboard Genoa sheet off the deck and it had wrapped itself around the starboard prop, the other end was still attached to the sail. Fortunately, we had not run the engines to charge the batteries, as this was usually a day time job, so we managed to retrieve the one end, but we could not do anything about the bit around the prop until the weather calmed down. It was a good thing we had two engines, so we were able to still use the port one for charging the batteries.

We found that because of the hard work the autopilot had to do driving Soñadora through those heavy seas that the batteries required 2/3 hours charging per day. Just imagine having to man the wheel in that weather for several days with only the two of us. Thank goodness for two engines, and the autopilot. It was like having 2 extra crew members. It was another lesson in seamanship, making sure there were no loose ropes on deck.

Some of the meat in the freezer had started to defrost, and we could not work out why. So we have had to have roast beef twice in one week. Shame! The meat from Gibraltar was pretty tough, and the fresh vegetables were not lasting as long as they should have, but I managed to bake some packet bread with success, and a couple of cakes.

On the sixteenth there was a moderate gale, force 7 with N/ E winds, variable, gusting to 38 knots? It eased off just long enough for us to change down sails. About 4.30 am the gales really hit us. Ron had to take the wheel again; the rain was so heavy that it was flattening the spray on top of the waves. But we were still making good time and reached our 2000 nm's.

The N/E trade winds seem to have settled at last. Blowing a steady 18/25 knots. What a difference! A pity we couldn't have had them sooner, though the rough squally weather had given us the much needed experience. We can now put the poles up and down in the dark, or in storms, and with 1,200 sq. foot of sail to handle, plus a swinging pole while balancing on a pitching deck, takes some doing. We were definitely getting better, ha-ha and so we should, we had just clocked 2,600 nm.

19th December 1976 it was Sunday we had finished cleaning up the white painted areas in the cockpit, and had polished all the stainless steel and scrubbed the teak. Soñadora looked really good, the cleanest she had ever been. Just as we had finished, a flying fish landed on the deck, it was a beautiful light royal blue. I threw it back into the sea, but it had left its calling card of a few scales on my nice clean deck!

We had another visitor, a small blue backed yellow tailed bird which flew into our starboard cabin through the open hatch, into the saloon and took up residence for the night on the book shelf. He was obviously from the islands but too far out at sea to have the strength to get back. Unfortunately, he had also brought some other visitors some quite large lice, which required a heavy dose of insect exterminator.

Late afternoon on the 20th December Ron had just finished working out our position and shouted to me, if we looked we could just about see Antigua. It was a truly great feeling. Unfortunately, we were too far off to decide exactly where we were, and as some parts of the coast have very nasty reefs it was too late in the evening to approach. So we put up the storm jib, and laid a hull and spent the worst night at sea of the trip so far. I didn't sleep a wink. Soñadora didn't like the short sharp beam seas' it was so bad even Ron didn't sleep!

It was a good thing that we had stood off for the night, as we found we were at the top end of Antigua, where most of the reefs are. We had a really good sail down the coast arriving at English Harbour at 14-00 hrs. We dropped anchor near the beach of Shirley Heights, opposite the hotel, Holiday Inn. Barry off Lady Jane and Bill Bullimore, now Captain of Anne Marie, were anchored close by and came over to welcome us. What a lovely surprise! Remember Bill came with us as crew when we sailed from Bristol on our 1,000 n.m qualifying trip for the Whitbread Multi-hull 1975 race which was unceremoniously cancelled.

Bill took Ron ashore to book in, as it was getting late, and the Port office would be closing. He arranged with Ron to meet us later at the Admirals Inn, just for drinks as he would be working till 10pm. The wharf was about 4 minutes away by motor boat. He also arranged for us thankfully to leave our meat in another yacht's freezer until morning, as it was beginning to defrost.

Normally you had to wait for the officials to come out to your yacht before going ashore, but Bill had told Ron that we would be waiting for ever as the outboard motor of the officials boat had packed up while going out to another yacht when the weather was rough. The officers couldn't row, and were going round in circles, being carried out to sea, getting more panic stricken by the minute. They were eventually rescued by a yachtsman. After this they had not gone out to a single Yacht. Apparently one poor Yacht had waited patiently for two days.

English Harbour in December 1976

Chapter 14   At Last Christmas in the Sun

On their return Bill and Ron were laughing their heads off. After Bill had left, Ron told me of the hilarious conversation that had taken place between him and the Port Officer, who spoke in a very cross broad Caribbean accent:

Port Officer   Man, you should have waited for me to visit you.

Ron   Yes I know, but I hear your outboard is broken so I have come to you.

Port Officer   You got Johnson out board?

R   No, I am rowing.

P/O   I can't come if you have no outboard

R   I know that is why I have come to you

P/O   you should wait for me to visit you.

R   I know but you have no outboard so you cannot come to me.

And so it went on, until all of a sudden he said" You got Johnny Walker whisky ? "No" said Ron. A look of sheer horror came over the officer's face so Ron quickly said "but we have Bells."

P/O   Dat good Whisky?

R   Very good, would you like a bottle?

P/O   You sure is good?

R   Very good

P/O   You got cigarettes?

R   Yes I will bring you some of those as well

After which it was smiles all round, and the clearance went smoothly. Over drinks with Bill he told us about the vagaries of Caribbean life, and life in general. Since we had last seen Bill, sadly his Sister had died shortly after he had left us in Southampton, I am convinced even today that if he had been able to stay with us we would never have got embayed in the Bay of Biscay, and would have got to the Caribbean as first planned.

After Bill had gone Ron blew up our dinghy, and took our meat over to the yacht Tarragona With thanks a great relief.

When Ron came back we finished sorting out the freezer, had dinner and went over to the Admirals Inn. This in Lord Nelson's days, used to be the load cellar and engineers offices.

To the right of the main gate was the guard house at the rear of which was the Police station where Ron had to leave our gun (standard regulation) and give the Officer his Christmas present of 2 bottles of whisky and the cigarettes.

The station used to be the Masters shipwright house beyond which was an upgraded site, which also included a large boathouse which was destroyed in an earthquake in 1843.

We had just sat down with our drinks, trying to accept the fact that we were actually on dry land and at anchor in one of the prettiest harbours I had seen up to that time, when a group of Islanders came into the Lounge Bar and started to sing Christmas Carols for about one hour. It could not have been a better way to spend our first night ashore, after three weeks at sea. They sang the songs the Caribbean way, swaying to the rhythm of the music, one in particular called O Holy Night. It was sung with such great feeling and charm and has been a favourite of ours ever since. We were very tired, so after the singing had ended and as Bill had not arrived, we returned to Soñadora, and slept like logs.

The next morning we were up and ashore by 9.30, looking for a fridge engineer, as the yacht we had left our meat on was leaving that day. Fortunately, we were able to store the meat quite cheaply at the local Nicholson's shop, who also recommended a fridge freezer engineer.

He came at 14-00 hrs, and de-gassed and re-gassed the freezer unit, and put in a new drier. Apparently moisture had got into the system. The total cost was an expensive £30 Oh woe is us! But at least the freezer was working.

We went to get our post, which cheered us up. We had cards and letters from all the family and friends in UK. Australia, New Zealand, Gibraltar, and Santander. We also had a card from St. John's post office, to say we had a parcel from Agua Marine. Hopefully this meant that our efforts in Las Palmas, had not been in vain, and our replacement instruments had at last arrived.

It was great getting post, and usually such fun opening it, though sometimes it could be frustrating and sad. One way or another there was little that could be done about it. I am not sure communications are any easier today, despite all the high-tech systems available. The best things about them are that the post doesn't physically get stolen, and is quicker. We had a quiet evening and went to bed at 21.00 hrs.

The next day was another early start. We got the meat back on board, had a good cooking session making stews and curries out of the tough steaks. At 14-00 hrs we caught the local bus, firstly into Falmouth harbour, a lovely wide shallow bay but not very good for long term anchorage having no facilities, and is exposed to the weather. We checked for post at the local post office but no luck, that day. However we did meet Stewart off Shangri-La again. Over a drink he told us that he had been in Antigua for a week and really liked it. He had come via Barbados, which he did not like, but thought that Falmouth Harbour was lovely.

We then went on into St John's arriving at the main post office at 15.25pm only to be told they were closing. They gave us a letter from Ron's Mother, but would not give us the parcel saying that we would have to come back in the morning. They were most unfriendly, we were not much impressed. The Town itself was very dilapidated and dirty, with the roads and buildings falling apart. We did manage to get our money changed, and decided to come back to the harbour by bus. We found the bus service to be very efficient, and funny, it was a lovely trip through the countryside taking about an hour because of the diversions. The bus took people almost to their doors if they have a lot of parcels to carry. Very accomodating. The bus was a transit van size, and squeezed in as many people as they could, all in good humour and it only cost 80 c.

The sad thing at that time was that the Island had recently gained its independence and most of the people gave the impression that they, didn't think they should have to work or give good service to anyone, not even their own, with the exception of the bus service. At first we thought their aggressive attitude to service was only towards the Europeans, but after watching them keeping their own people waiting in shops to be served we realised it was their general behaviour.

We got back before dark and we decided to invite Barry and Marion to dinner. I was going to cook roast beef which is an easy meal to share. Bill and his girlfriend came later for drinks. He told us that he had left his wife, also, that his sister had died since he was last with us on the   Soñadora. Barry expanded on the problems he had experienced with his crew coming from Gibraltar, which had really begun to spoil his enjoyment of the cruising life. We were so glad we didn't need crew. All in all we had a happy evening.

On Christmas Eve, 24th December 1976 Ron got up early and went into St John's to collect our parcel, while I cleaned through the boat, and organised for the laundry to be done by Maud, a big happy islander, for only £3. Then I got ready for Christmas day by doing some last minute shopping, finding the food very expensive compared to UK and not good quality.

Ron returned in time for lunch, with the parcel and some more post. He had had a lot of hassle getting the parcel from the customs at the post office. The letters were from Trevor and his Mother, they were both full of woe as Queenie, mothers neighbour had, had a stroke, food and rates had gone up and the weather was freezing cold! Ron had posted our mail off to UK NZ and AU. But only cards, letters would follow later as I had not had the time to write more. Post became very important as time went by.

Carole, Ron, Stanley and Eithne Mann

After lunch I swam ashore to the lovely beach opposite to where Soñadora was anchored and near the Holiday Inn. There I met a very nice youngish London couple, Stanley and Eithne Mann. We arranged to meet up later at the Admirals Inn, where Ron had also arranged to meet another couple, Robert and Sylvia Wells, off their yacht Sylvia from California USA, also Barry and Marion, Bill and his girlfriend. We had a great Christmas Eve, swapping stories, listening to the steel band, in the warm tropical atmosphere.

CHRISTMAS IN THE SUN 1976

We had made it, and it was wonderful our dream had come true. We went to bed very happy.

December 25th, we had been invited to meet up with everyone for a Champagne Breakfast, starting at 10.00am. As we had overslept we didn't get there until 11.00am when it was nearly over. The group was fairly merry and some were trying to sing Carols without music, not so well.

Robert having got bored with this was trying to fire his foot long model cannon, and being disappointed in the result started to try and fire the real one on the quayside, there was no stopping him! Ron thought it was getting dangerous, so we went over to the Admirals Inn, with Barry and Marion, as they had booked Christmas lunch there. We came back to Soñadora, wished her a Happy Christmas and thanked her for keeping us safe.

We filled up a flask of gin and tonic for Ron and one with whisky and water for me, picked up the radio and towels, rowed ashore and had a lovely long afternoon swimming, climbing and sunbathing, returning to Soñadora, just before the sun went down. We cooked our festive dinner, and enjoyed the quietest Christmas we had ever had. Poor Bill was not with us as he had had to set sail at midday. He and his crew were not very thrilled about it, but that was what the owners wanted, no doubt they had been saved a hangover!

Boxing Day was a lazy day; we got up late, had a good breakfast, filled our flasks as before and went ashore to the yacht club to see the Christmas yacht race. We were too early so Ron brought a drink and settled down to listen to the music. I was restless, all this sleep and rest didn't agree with me, so I went for a swim and a walk.

On my way back to Ron, to watch the race, I met up

with two single hander's, (people who sail on their own long distances) Stewart and James off Salt Dragon, and they walked back with me. We spent a very pleasant three hours watching the racing, swopping stories and listening to the music. Then Ron and I spent another quiet evening on board Soñadora. I understand that these days at English Harbour, there are so many yachts now at Christmas that you couldn't have a quiet time even if you wanted it.

27th December 1976 we were visited by Stanley and Eithne for coffee, and then Glyn Mason off the yacht Rata, a Nantucket Clipper, came into the harbour. We had met him in Puerto Rico, the Canaries, he was sailing single handed. After he had dropped anchor we rowed him ashore to get clearance and buy him a much needed drink at the Admirals Inn. He had left the Canaries the day before us, it had taken him 37 days and he looked very well.

We all went back to Soñadora, Stewart also came over to introduce his brother Grant, who had just arrived by plane from New Zealand. Everyone joined us for an early dinner, and to catch up with the news, then Glyn left early to get some much needed sleep, shortly after which the others left, so we also had an early night.

The next day we went ashore to meet up with Eithne to do some shopping. While we were in the shop, there was a French couple having trouble, not being able to pay with their franks. The shop wasn't a bit helpful. It was too late to get to the bank in St.John's, so I offered to lend them $20, but in the end Eithne gave it to them.

We met up with Ron, Bob, and Glyn, at the Admirals Inn for drinks and had a lovely afternoon. Bob invited Ron and me to spend the evening on his yacht, but we had already accepted an invitation to spend it with Stanley and Eithne at their hotel, so we had one more drink with Bob, then we dropped Eithne off at the Hotel and Glyn back to his yacht to get changed, then the three of us had dinner on Soñadora, before going up to the hotel to join Eithne and Stanley. We had a very enjoyable evening, seeing how the holiday makers were entertained. It was great fun.

The following day after I had just returned from my swim we were visited by the French family, Max, Claude, and Maria, off yacht Pimpirinak of Bayonne. They had come to return the money they had borrowed. We had coffee, and they left, having invited us to join them on their yacht the following evening for rum punches. After which Bob came aboard, to go over the charts with Ron, also Stanley and Eithne came. I gave her the $20, which I think she was surprised to get back, although I wasn't. Then we all went to Bob's yacht Sylvia for the rest of the evening. They were a very nice couple, and Bob told some great stories. As they were leaving early the next morning, we returned to Soñadora for an early night.

Bob and Sylvia were bound for the Grenadines, the Windward Islands, at the bottom end of the Caribbean. We shall miss them. You meet a lot of people in this cruising life, some you take to instinctively and really miss them when they go, others are great fun and you are happy in their company, and glad to meet up with them again. Thank goodness there are only a very few that are not really nice to know, but I never really got used to saying good bye. It is one of the sad parts of cruising. Ron used to laugh at me and turn it into a joke.

That evening as arranged we went on Pimpirinak F21H she was a lovely 44ft Ketch built in Taiwan. On board we met another French couple Bernard and Irene Campagnac with their lovely young daughter Valerie. Irene was a stamp collector and Bernard a Radio Ham operator, and very interesting to talk to. Their yacht, a 35footer, was unusually named with his call sign F21H. They had come from Uhartcheverria, Urrugne in France.

The rum punches must have been very strong because on the way back to Soñadora, Ron said something which upset me, and caused a row, when we got back on board. This was most unusual for us, so I went to bed in a huff. Usually our arguments are a two minute blast on both sides, and then it was all over. We are usually very compatible at sea, more so than on land.

New Years Eve Glyn, came on board and we decided that a long walk would be good for us. So up to Shirley Heights we went, a hill south east of the dock yard, and the easiest way up not wanting to make life too hard would be over to the beach and up through the back of the Holiday Inn. I swam ashore, and had a shower in Eithne's room while the boys brought the dinghy over.

Left to Right Joseph (Leo), Barry, Marion, Carole and Ron 7-1-1977

At the top of Shirley Heights are the last vestiges of the fort's military barracks. The view across the bay was beautiful, clear blue waters, golden sands, and lush tropical foliage. Just how we had pictured a Tropical Island to be while sitting in our armchairs in a freezing rainy UK. What a great way to spend the last day of the year!

We returned to Soñadora for lunch, and then Glyn went back to his yacht for a siesta in preparation to celebrate the New Year. We picked him up again at eight o'clock and went to the Admirals Inn, where the people from Primpiriank F21H, and Stanley and Eithne were waiting for us. We all gave a really great welcome to the New Year of 1977 dancing to the wonderful sounds of the steel band. Much to our surprise this finished at one thirty a.m. so as Max had some champagne we all retired to Soñadora. (So she didn't feel left out)! And continued to have the best evening of the trip so far, finishing about four thirty.

New Years Day, 1977 we had a very slow start which was no surprise! I had a practice with Barry's snorkeling gear, but couldn't get on with it at all, though Ron found it OK. Glyn came to lunch and we had a very quiet but pleasant day.

The second of January there was the traditional local and visitors yacht race, and we had invited Stanley and Eithne and Glyn to come for a sail. We had thought to join in the race, but the winds were so light we gave up and just went for a sail where the winds would take us. Had we given it a bit more thought we could have sailed around to Falmouth Bay, anchored for lunch and sailed back, but we hadn't quite got our act together, nor were we fully recovered from the continuous celebrations. We were not complaining, but Ron was disappointed that we couldn't show off Soñadora's prowess to our guests. When we got back we anchored closer to the quay, so that we didn't have so far to row. As Stanley and Eithne were flying back to London that evening, Eithne gave me her snorkeling gear. It fitted me better than Barry's did, though I

Shirley Heights looking out to sea and back into the hills

have never been much good at using it.

We went over to the Holiday Inn to have a farewell drink, we were sorry to see them go, as they had been such good company. Having bid them a good flight home the three of us went back to the Admirals Inn. Glyn was very happy the whole day, as he had had a letter from his girl friend in Wales whom he was hoping would come out and join him, and possibly sail with him across the Pacific. He was so impressed with how happy Ron and I and other sailing couples that he had met were. He just couldn't wait for her to join him, and we wished him luck. As a result he got a bit drunk and insulted an Irishman! Bad move! We smoothed it over, I have forgotten the cause, but it was funny because at first sight of him I had thought he was a woman, I think it was his long hair. (It wouldn't have raised an eyebrow today). I couldn't have been more wrong! Fortunately, he didn't know this or there would have been no friendly result.

We also met an American named Conrad who had a 44ft. Ketch steel yacht, he used to be an air pilot, and he invited us to visit him the following day.

3rd January 1977. Our new anchorage though closer to the quay was not so good for swimming but good for getting ashore when the wind was up as it often was. We visited Conrad, and were most impressed with his Monohull yacht. It had a large saloon, three heads and showers, a very well appointed galley and his coffee was good! He mainly motor sailed her, and seemed able to take her to most places, even up the French canals. He had also been to Dominica and liked it. This was where Ron was thinking we would go to next. It is a couple of islands down from Antigua.

Barry and Marion came over to us for lunch, and told us about all the terrible problems they had had since   building their yacht, things kept going wrong. They couldn't sail it by themselves and they couldn't find good crew. The crew that had come with them from Gibraltar had speedily left, so they were unable to continue sailing to other islands. They really enjoyed harbour life, but had come to hate sailing. To me this seemed a pity after all their work. Ron was sympathising with them, saying he found the ocean crossings, about 95% boring and 5% sheer terror, and was so pleased we didn't need crew. Though this did mean it was a lot of work for the two of us as Soñadora was not completely finished, but was still very comfortable to live on.

No sooner had they gone than Conrad visited us, bringing his American and Swedish crew. They were a   pleasant young couple and they all seemed to get on well, and had had a good trip so far.

Once we were on our own, I asked Ron how he really felt about sailing in general, now that we had made one ocean crossing, and had a better understanding of the work involved. He after all took the major responsibility. I was able to help him with the deck work, as well as the cooking and cleaning inside, but I am still not an engineer or a navigator, so I thought, that if he was finding it too much, we could sell her, and continue by plane. He had nothing to prove to anyone, and that while I loved the life at sea nobody really knew if they would, until they had tried it. It could be very hard going and no fun unless we both enjoyed it most of the time. Ron's response was "Carole I said I was going to sail her around the world, and sail her around we shall! So don't worry, we are doing ok. But thanks for the thought." Ron can be very stubborn, but I felt better for having asked the question, because once we went through the Panama Canal and into the Pacific, there was no ducking out.

4th January 1977 we went ashore to say good bye to Brazil Champion, from the yacht Pollack. He was a New Zealander, from Auckland, whom we had first met in Gibraltar. He was now bound for the Virgin Islands.

We had a good laugh over coffee, as he told us one of his

many tales. This one was about the time when he was coming through the Suez Canal and into the Mediterranean. He had managed to get thrown into an Arab Prison twice in one night, which has to be a record for any yachtsman. He not only got in but also out, twice! I forget the reason. Only a New Zealander could be so lucky.

On our return we went for a swim, and I tried out Eithne's snorkeling gear, it worked very well, Oh what a hard life this was! But we were getting restless as all our friends were sailing away, so Ron suggested that we sailed down to Dominica and invite Barry, Marion, and Glyn along. I was surprised and pleased at the same time. They happily accepted so we spent the next day in preparation. This would be the start of our cruise of the Caribbean Islands

5th January 1977. We moored stern to the quay to take on water, and were helped by some very nice crew   members from Senator Teddy Kennedy's yacht Currish which happened to be alongside us. They were getting ready for his arrival tomorrow.

It took us hours to get the water, as there were 6 yachts ahead of us. However while we were waiting we were approached by a personable young man called Leo who asked Ron if we would give him a lift as he lived on Dominica Island. He had come to Antigua looking for work, but there was none, so he wanted to go home but couldn't   afford the fare. We said that this was o.k. but that we wouldn't be going until the next day and it would be a night sail but leaving at midday

The freezer engineer came aboard and changed the drier yet again, costing us another $40. He said he was sure it would be ok now. He seemed genuine.

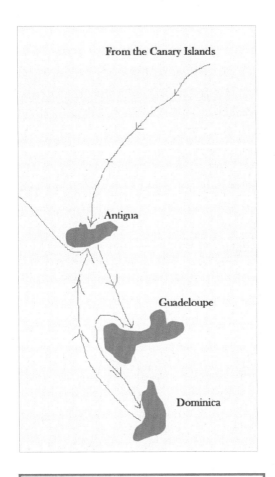

A short cruise in the Caribbean

Chapter 15   A Short Cruise in the Carribbean

We went ashore for our last minute shopping. We picked up "Joseph" known as "Leo" who straight away, changed out of his good clothes into working ones, and offered to help Ron. We took this as a very good sign. As soon everyone was aboard, we set sail at 1pm. The weather was good with a brisk wind. It was great being at sea again and everyone soon settled down. I cooked dinner, and it was decided that the men would do the night watch between them.

The next day we awoke to a cloudy, squally day Leo was sea sick, which surprised me. It was amazing just how many islanders were, and as we discovered, it was just the same throughout the Pacific.

Dominica Island kept disappearing behind the rain clouds, and we eventually arrived about 5pm. We had taken the sails down and were motoring. As we entered the lovely wide Prince Rupert bay, with palm trees all around the edge of golden sands, and up the hills as far as one could see.

Three small canoes manned by three small boys came up behind us paddling very hard to keep up with Soñadora riding the wakes of her two hulls, wanting a tow in. Leo took their lines, it was great fun.

Once we had anchored the boys wanted to order taxies for trips around the Island, and boats to take us up the Indian River and to order baskets of fruit. They were expert's at pressure selling, and it wasn't until Leo appeared and told them that he was looking after us that they went away, though we had all enjoyed their tow in.

Ron took Leo ashore accompanied by Barry to clear customs, no problems, it only cost $7.50, and we could stay as long as we liked with no bribe required. There were no facilities, but we didn't need any so that was ok. I cooked dinner, and Marion helped by insisting on washing up after every meal, we had a   pleasant evening, retiring early.

9th January 1977. Leo arrived early laden down with fresh bananas, coconuts and grapefruits, the best we had seen since being in the Caribbean. He wouldn't take anything for them, so I ask if I could give him something for his mother, he was very modest and only asked for a bottle of wine, which we gladly gave to him.

We all went ashore about 12 midday. Leo took us up the main street, which was in a very poor state considering that the British had only just granted them their independence, the roads, pavements, and facilities in general were a disgrace to our government, Leo's parent's home was at the end of the village, small but very clean and tidy, his Mother a really nice woman, obviously took a great pride in her home and family, and she looked a lot younger than his seventy two year old father. He gave the impression of having been a bit of a reprobate in his time, he was very amusing. Leo's Sister Joan was the local school teacher, and stated that the level of education was equal to any. They all made us very welcome, and seemed to have a happier outlook on life than the Antiguans. Perhaps because they didn't have so much tourism.

Joan gave me some christophines, light greenish yellow fine prickly 5 inch pear shaped vegetables, with instructions on how to cook them, and they were indeed quite tasty.

Leo then came back to the dinghy with us escorted by a small boy, Leo asked if we would take him as guide up the Indian river, while he looked after Soñadora for us, the young boy only wanted $5, who could refuse, though really with three strong men. We hardly needed him, but he was happy so were we.

There was quite a swell at the entrance to the river, and Ron had to maneuver a way through the many small steel cargo tugs, we motored on up the river about 2-3 miles, it was like a picture straight out of a Tarzan film, long vines hanging from the mango type trees into the river, with snatched views of banana plants and coconut trees behind them. The only thing missing were the crocodiles or as far as I could find out anything remotely dangerous or poisonous.

The river was beautifully clear and quite cool, reaching depths of 5-8 ft. there wasn't a lot of light we felt like explorers of the Amazon. It made us realise just how quickly you could get lost in the jungle, however, not here on the island, though it did give you an eerie feeling. We came across a rapid, and had to get out and carry the dinghy over it, (no blood sucking leaches thank goodness) our wild imaginings gave us plenty of laughter.

On the second bend we met a woman and two men on their way back in their dinghy, their yacht was anchored the other side of the Island. While we were talking, Alvin had gone off into the trees, and came back with some fresh coconuts, which we shared with them. They then continued on their way home, while we carried on until we met another set of rapids, the river was very shallow, so we decided we had had enough of playing Tarzan, we enjoyed lunch and started on our return. This time we paddled, it was magic, so peaceful, Peter kept Alvin amused all the way, and we all had a great time.

We got back to Soñadora, had a cup of tea, a short rest, and then went ashore again, this time walking towards the south of the Island. As we went along Barry was chatting to some children, and asked them to take us to where we could get some bananas. They took us to a plantation, but it didn't seem right to Ron just to help yourself, so, Barry went and paid the boys $2.

On the way back we stopped at a wooden shack and bought some ginger beer, and some very soggy donuts, I couldn't eat them, but a little girl standing by was delighted to have them.

We had just started back when a Geest Banana truck

pulled up and asked Ron if he liked bananas, and how was he going to eat them. Ron not quite knowing what to say, answered "wait until they get ripe," "that's right" said the driver, and drove off, much to Ron's relief and everyone else's. It could have been difficult, we returned to Soñadora had dinner watching the sun go down, another good day.

The following morning while we were having breakfast in the cockpit, a young Dominican came along side in his canoe asking for money, he looked so thin I said I would cook him a bacon and egg sandwich which he said he would take to his family, I said no he must eat it, and I would make him another one to take home. Which he happily did, plus a goody bag.

Barry started to make some very scathing remarks about my gullibility until Ron said that if we couldn't share our breakfast with a child what was this life all about.

The trio decided that they wanted to hitch hike to Roseau, south of the Island, in spite of being warned by the police that if we did hire a car, to watch out for the "Dreads" Islanders who lived in the back forests, smoked pot, and attacked strangers with machetes, and if we did see any of them, not to stop, but to run them down if necessary, and tell him how many we had knocked down on return. Quite a thought! The trio wouldn't share a taxi or hire car, and Ron didn't want to go by bus. The roads were very bad and two hours of hard bumping up and down jammed up against a lot of hot sweaty bodies, while sitting on hard seats, wasn't Ron's idea of fun, he also didn't like hitch hiking.

We stayed behind and had a very enjoyable day, visiting the 'Spot Light' and 'Purple Turtle' clubs, neither of which was up to much, with dirt floors, bamboo walls not very clean, and very expensive for that time, $1.50 per drink of any sort, but they were very friendly.

We also went for a walk to Douglas Bay, which was really

nice, but not very good for swimming as the surf was too strong that the first ten foot of water was full of sand.

On returning to Soñadora we found the trio had returned and were not very enthusiastic about their trip. We suggested that they might like to go to the 'Spot Light' club that evening, but their sense of enjoyment seemed to be at a very low ebb.

11th January 1977 we were all ashore by 7.30am having arranged with Leo to take us to the local market. When we got there only a few people had anything to sell, but nothing that interested us, so we left some money with Leo to see what he could get for us, and returned to Soñadora for breakfast with the idea that if Leo returned on time we would leave. He was late, but came with two dozen grapefruit, three cucumbers, eight onions, and a stork of bananas, all for $8 we were very pleased.

Leo stayed for a leisurely lunch, we wished him good luck and thanked him for being such a good crew member. Ron rowed him ashore.

We had decided to move across the bay and anchored opposite the 'Star Light' club, while running the engines to charge the batteries and freeze the deep freeze down.

The trio decided that they were only going to look at the club and not buy a drink, which we thought was a bit mean, and they didn't want to wait until Ron had finished running the engines, so they went ashore on the understanding that Ron and I would join them later.

As it was they didn't go to the club but motored off along the coast, obviously with no intentions of waiting for us, which upset me, and made me wish they would run out of petrol and have a long row back, but no such luck. Fortunately, before they got back, yacht happy sailing club Nordestern came in and anchored close by. We had met the owner Mannin a German in Gibraltar under very amusing circumstances. In the dark one of his crew tripped and   fell   into the water in Gibraltar harbour. We had rescued him,   gave him a hot shower before he went back to his boat taking a pair of my knickers with him by mistake. Returning them in the morning very red faced from the ragging his friends were giving him.

This time Mannin only had one crew with him, an 18 year old Dominican who he was taking back to Germany to his family to help him find a job, what a lucky young man, let's hope it all worked out.

Mannin had been lucky on his trip to Dominica, he had found a power boat floating upside down way out at sea, with a good engine, worth about £2000, we had left before we heard the results of his reporting it to the local police, he was hoping to be able to claim "salvage at sea", on it, for those who are unaware of the meaning, if you find something at sea and get your rope on to it for towing to bring it safely home, you could be eligible to keep it all, or part of it's cargo, the Captain getting 50% and the rest divided amongst the crew, (just as the pirates and navy share riggers did only 100 years ago). Depending on whether it is a company ship or privately owned.

We were all invited over to his boat for drinks etc., then we returned for dinner to Soñadora, Mannin didn't want to come as he already had his prepared, but he joined us later for coffee, a very enjoyable evening.

Seven am. Found us departing Dominica bound for Guadeloupe arriving about five pm. We had had some rough weather, and then calms, ending up motoring in, the information we had been given about where to report in was incorrect, and we were to late anyway, the local bar wouldn't change our money into franks, so it was back to Soñadora, a good meal and an early night.

We had had a good look at the immediate village though

and were most impressed with everything we saw. The roads and buildings were beautifully maintained, and every one appeared to be well dressed, unlike Dominica, which made us feel ashamed at how poorly the British Government had looked after their colonies, the French of course call their colonies "Departments of France," and govern them wherever they are as a complete extension of France, policed by police from France and not by the locals, which obviously made a difference to investors, and the Island as a whole.

We got to the customs office to report in at 10am. No one was there, for some reason this caused an argument between Ron, Barry and Glyn, so we went to the police station, they were very helpful, and told us not to worry we could sign in on our way back. Again we could not get our money changed anywhere, so feeling very irritated with things in general, we all decided to catch the local bus into Pointe-A-Pitre, a one and a half hour trip. The mini bus was extremely comfortable and clean, with delightful music much needed, which cheered Ron and I up. The ride through the country was lovely, the roads were well surfaced, and the houses, even the poorer type ones were built on concrete bases, nowhere did we see the poverty and disrepair of buildings that we did on Dominica. The Islanders appeared to be well dressed and confident in their outlook, with very little unemployment, I said to Ron, that as an Islander I would rather have been under French rule than British, and that included Antigua, Ron reminded me that the French Islanders would never get independence, which the British islands now had, and probably preferred that, even in their poverty, only time would tell.

When we arrived we indicated to the driver that we had to get to the bank before we could pay him, he wasn't too pleased at this, but must have been used to it from yacht people, because he just called a boy over to take us to the bank, which again was closing for lunch, but they did point out a hotel that would help us, which they did, thank goodness. Ron paid and tipped the driver, so he was pleased, we left him smiling, always a good thing. We all went back to the hotel for a much needed beer, and hopefully lunch.

We discovered that we only had enough money for a beer each and a plate of chips. The trio went back to the bank again, and Ron and I went to look around town. It was a mistake having an odd number on board it split us into two groups, it would have worked with one or two of them, but not three a pity really, but at least we have found out what we had wondered about, not to take crew unless there were extenuating circumstances.

We all met up again at the bus station, Barry paid Ron the money back he had borrowed and we had an enjoyable ride home, again the music was great. Barry still hadn't got a good word to say about the French, even though when we got to the local bar, and were told that we didn't have to clear customs.

Ron suggested to Barry that we stay and have a drink to show international good will, and may be make it easier for other British yachts coming after us, which one always tries to think about, but no they wouldn't so we spent the last of our coinage on wine and beer, keeping the 10 frank note, for future use. Returning to Soñadora we spent a pleasant evening in spite of everything.

We departed at six am under engine power. I had really liked Guadeloupe, but was looking forward to getting back to Antigua, I heard the men putting up the mainsail while I made the tea, then I went back to bed, to doze.

I was almost asleep when I heard a commotion on deck, so up I got again. We had caught a lobster pot rope around our port engine propeller. Fortunately, the engine wasn't running, as nothing could be done about it for now, we had breakfast and a good sail back. Glyn surprisingly paid Ron $30 for the trip, even though he had brought some stores with him.

It was great to be back in Antigua. We had letters from Trevor, Mother and Yvonne my sister in Australia, all with good news. Marco Landolt's schooner, Astragalae was in, but we didn't see him, everyone was busy getting their yachts ready to leave. We hadn't seen anything of Lady Jane and Barry and Marion, not even for them to say thank you for the trip, which didn't surprise us. We were beginning to realise that there were a few users and takers in the yachting world, as everywhere else. Fortunately, we didn't meet many as we went along our way.

We went into St. John's, to the British Consul to find out if we needed a US Visa to go to the American Caribbean Is. and were told no. We owned our own yacht and had no crew, so we were ok. We then went looking for a water pump and starter solenoid, but failed to get either. In the process though we did meet a very friendly, jolly six foot Islander who drove us around in his car to look for them. He wouldn't take anything for his trouble, saying he was so sorry he had not succeeded. Happy moments!

We then went to the Shipwreck restaurant for a steak. Ron's was tough and the waiter overheard Ron complaining to me about it. To our pleasant surprise they presented Ron with another one, which was very good. It was the first time I had ever known Ron to complain about food as he had got such strong teeth and could usually eat through anything.

Back on board that evening, Glyn came over to see us, and told us that quite a few yachts were going in convoy up to the Northern Islands, and as he still had three weeks to wait before his girlfriend joined him he thought he would go, and would we go also? I think he was hoping we would and ask him to join us, but we were not ready yet to move again. We wished him luck but in the end he did not go either.

John Quinn, skipper of Ocean Clare came over to invite us to see his yacht, a lovely vessel, as it should be for the quarter of a million it cost to build. John, a delightful man of about thirty five years had a charter party on board bound for Guadeloupe. Ron gave him all the information he had and John reciprocated with information on the American Virgin Islands. Apparently, they are a good place to stock up, so we planned to eventually go there. Unfortunately, when we did go, we were turned away as we did not have a visa. This was despite the fact that we were told by the British Consulate in Antigua that we didn't need one.

We then went for a walk up to the remains of Berkeley Fort which overlooked the harbour. There was just a solitary cannon and the footings of the powder house. It was noticeably quiet, with beautiful views. We called in at the Admirals Inn, on our way home and met up with Glyn who wanted to swap a chart for some dry stores. What a lovely day!

Looking from Berkeley Fort across the harbour

The next day was a work day. Ron was busy trying to repair the instruments again without success and I was making a bikini for myself and some shorts for Ron.

On the twentieth, Marion came over to say goodbye, but made no mention of returning hospitality. At least she came. She did tell us about the concrete yacht, Lilly Maid, which was a wandering store ship, and the skipper sold fish to other yachts. We also learned that he was divorced, but was still friendly with his ex. All of life was there! We were then visited by James off Salt Dragon, which was up on the slipway having some work done. James, an interesting man just wanted to swap some books and have a coffee.

21st January 1977. I could hardly believe my eyes! Barry has just sailed away without so much as a wave or a nod of the head. Glyn sailed over to say goodbye and to tell us they were going to Green Island for a couple of days, and would see us on their return. I wished them fair winds. When I told Ron about Barry and Marion's departure he just laughed and said "Good, now we can move Soñadora closer to the quay."

We then went in the dinghy to the slipway to visit James and gave him some bananas. Then on to visit John Martin on his 45ft. Polynesian Wagram design catamaran. He needed all the room for two adults and five children. The children loved it but his wife wasn't too keen, but agreed that it sailed well.

They had just got rid of their crew, and were lucky to do so. John had given them their air fares back to the UK, only to discover that they hadn't bought flight tickets, but had spent the money on other things! John had to get the police to escort them to the next plane, and he had to buy more tickets. He warned us that the captain of a yacht is responsible for the crew and they cannot be discharged just anywhere. They have to be flown back to where they came from, unless you have a legal agreement with them before hand. John had not known this, and neither had we. He had only taken them on, out of the goodness of his heart, thinking it would be a good experience for two young lads. It was a costly lesson, for like us John didn't have a lot of money to spare.

We then went on to collect our post and we had a card from Pauline and Ron off Samantha Jane, also a catamaran. We had met them in Southampton. They were now in Alicante, so we wouldn't be seeing them for a while, if ever.

I made some bread that day, but had to sieve the flour first as it had some weevils in it! I knew that people joked about weevils providing good protein, but I did not like them wiggling about in my flour. Fortunately, I had not got any more of that brand of flour. The bread was fine, thank goodness. The Martin family came to visit; the children were very well behaved and loved Soñadora.

The following day we were visited by Tony McLean. He had just come for morning coffee, but stayed for lunch, and eventually left about 5pm. He was so entertaining.

That is the beauty of this life. You have flexible time and can stop and enjoy company at any time of the day. Tony was ex RAF and looked the part, with his concrete yacht called Wee Pesky that he had just about built himself, with the help of his RAF and Scottish dock yard friends. He and the yacht complemented each other. He didn't wear a kilt, only shorts, with wide legs and no underpants! so that when he put a leg up to climb aboard all was revealed. You did not have to ask him if he would have worn anything under his kilt!

24th January 1977. Ron had stripped off the solenoid and water pump from the port engine, so we went into St. John's hoping to get spares. We had a very good day and got everything we needed except the seal for the water pump. We got back about 5pm. Ron decided not to put the engine back together again, until after he had got the pulley welded at the dock yard which was arranged for the next day at 4pm. By then the freezer would be slowly starting to defrost again.

The next day while Ron was getting the pulley welded, I went to get the post, and had a letter from Malcolm Hudson, (Gibraltar). It seems he had had a good Christmas, but had been ill, poor fellow. We had enjoyed his company so much, and it was really good to hear from him. I also met Tony who said he was off to Trinidad the next day, and would like us to come for drinks at about eight o'clock.

Ron re-installed the pulley and started the engine. Hopefully he had fixed the leaky pump, as the freezer was now freezing again. He also finished painting the engines. With a bit of luck all will be well this time.

We had a hilarious evening aboard Wee Pesky. Tony had also invited Peter, a Cornish man off yacht Free Ranger from Falmouth, UK. While we were all down below enjoying ourselves, we had not noticed the wind getting up and it had flipped Peter's dinghy over losing his oars. Luckily they had floated to the quay, and were easily retrieved. We always wedged our oars under the seat no matter how calm it looked, as the weather was very changeable and you cannot get far in a dinghy without oars or an outboard. We got back to Soñadora about 2.30 am still laughing.

26th January 1977. By the time we had got up both Peter and Tony had gone. I was sure they would have a wonderful time in Trinidad.

John Martin came by to tell us that he had just received from the UK a solenoid. It had cost a third more than the one we had got in St. John's so we had been lucky. Ron was busy putting starter switches for the engines just inside the main saloon door. It would be good at last to be able to start them from inside. I was busy reducing the size of a mattress, to fit the cockpit seats and washing the mould off the covers with Domestos. I spent the rest of the day writing letters which I enjoy.

Ron was also busy putting lights up in the cockpit. He was slowly putting more of the finishing touches to Soñadora. This was quite a lot of work for one man, whilst also sailing.

After lunch we went to the yacht club and met Mary and David Duerden, off yacht Varuna and Captain Aleck and Dorothy Slater, with their children, and also Alexandra and James who were on holiday staying at the Beach Apartments. They were from Nova Scotia, Canada and James invited us all to lunch the following day.

28th January 1977. We had a delicious lunch at James's apartment, where we were introduced to Daniel Sohklowsky off yacht Rhea, an Aristocat catamaran, and were invited for coffee the following morning.

The next morning when we arrived we found that to our surprise that his girlfriend Frances was topless! Being a nurse I was afraid she would get burnt as she was cooking with very hot splattering oil. I was very tempted to advise her to wear a bib apron when cooking, but decided that it must be her usual way, and pretended that we were quite used to seeing half naked women floating about the deck. Thank goodness when they came to Soñadora the following day she wore tops as well as bottoms.

For the next few days we were busy with boat maintenance. It was very pleasant. Aleck offered to help Ron and I take Soñadora over to Freemans Bay, where we could beach her and scrub her bottom. This was very hard work, as the goose neck barnacles were very thick and very well stuck. I think they must have used the precursor of Araldite glue. It was very good of Aleck and we all got back late afternoon exhausted.

1st February 1977. Aleck, Dorothy, Mary and David came to dinner. This started off very well, but deteriorated as the evening went on, as Aleck, upset every one with his fixed ideas about left wing politics. We had a real job to change the subject, but eventually we did, so the evening ended on a more pleasant note.

The next day we met a very nice South African family, Pete and Jean Boshoff, who with their young family had sailed in their yacht Islander from their home country. Unfortunately, they sailed south the next day. During the next few days work came to a stop, I was beginning to think that Ron did not want to go any further. He hadn't said anything, so I hoped I was wrong.

8th February 1977. We had just spent two days moored stern to in order to get the freezer fixed once again. It cost $50 = £12 (which seems very little at today's prices, but to us then it was expensive) this time we hoped it was fixed properly.

We shared a taxi with David and Mary, to go into St. Johns to get fresh stores. We had a great shop, and returned to have dinner aboard Varuna. It was roast lamb and very delicious. Mary was a good cook. Over dinner David told us that he was in the private airline business and had recently flown back from the UK, having had major surgery for a gastric ulcer. Though it very nearly cost him his life, it was a really funny story. It went something like this.

They had been in Antigua for only a short while when David collapsed, and was rushed to St. John's hospital, where, we were impressed that they had correctly diagnosed a bleeding gastric ulcer, stating that he would need an immediate blood transfusion, and operation. However they would not operate until the blood they were going to use on him was first replaced, pint for pint. If he died from loss of blood before it was replaced then that was too bad.

A quick call went out to all the yachts, and in no time the situation was resolved. David went to theatre, while Mary went back to Varuna to contact his company and asked them to come and rescue him and fly him back to the UK, as soon after the emergency operation as possible.

Meanwhile a few hours later David was recovering from the anaesthetic, and in his own words said "Whcn I opened my eyes I thought I had died and gone to hell, there was this goat's face looking at me. We stared eye ball to eye ball for several minutes, before I realised that it was a real goat, and I was alive, and in a bed in the general ward. Not only was there a goat, but chickens pecking away under my bed as well, I thought God, what has Mary done to me? I didn't think I was that bad as a husband!"

By this time we were all in hysterics. We knew   about African bush land care, and it was not much better in Antigua. Apparently when one member of the family goes into hospital the whole family moved in, including the animals if there was no one else to look after them.

David now looked very well, but it hadn't affected his lifestyle at all. His yacht was moored stern to the quay, and you could guarantee that if you walked passed it after 11am, David would be out on deck making up his drink for the day. This went as follows, into a round five gallon ice cool box went one bottle of vodka or gin, one of rum, and two bags of ice, and then it was topped up with fruit juice. If you wanted a sober day, you dare not walk by after late morning. David would call you over, and would almost drag you on board and your morning would be gone, but very pleasantly. No one complained too loudly.

9th February 1977. The next day while still tied to the quay Mary and David brought their children aboard for dinner. They were such well behaved children, mad keen on stamp collecting, so we found quite a few for them. It is a good occupation for children travelling around the world.

The next few days we spent preparing to leave for the Panama Canal. We went over to anchor at 'Freeman's Bay' to give

Soñadora's bottom another scrub. There was a good inch of growth, in only just ten days.

While we were there Aleck insisted that we came ashore to meet some new people. We rowed ashore, tied our dinghy to the wooden pier and were introduced to John and Brenda Taylor, and Roy and Brenda Lewis, off Talon, a large Ferro-cement yacht. They had built it as a joint effort, in Canada after having got on so well while building their house. They had just sailed down from Canada nonstop.

It was quite obvious that they had not enjoyed the venture, though they had not quite come to blows. This was in spite of the fact that they all appeared to be really nice people, and had planned to sail on to New Zealand.

It was such a shame after all that effort. We later learned that they had decided to separate and each couple would have the yacht for two years. One couple would continue on to NZ. While the other would fly back to Canada. They tossed for it and the Lewis's won. After this they became reasonably friendly again.

There is no doubt that a great test of a relationship would be to go to sea. If it survives a three to five week trip then it will survive anything.

When we decided to go back to our boat we discovered that the dinghy had been blown over, completely submerging the Seagull outboard. Ron had to row against a choppy sea making it hard work. He was not amused, as we were off to St Bart's, part of St. Martins Islands. that evening leaving at 5pm. We hoped the Seagull would be dried out by the time we got there.

We arrived at St Bart's Island at 10pm. The winds had made the sea very lively and had made me feel sea sick, in the same way as it had when we left Southampton. Fortunately, I could still do my watch and anything else required, you cannot afford to be sick when there are only two of you.

We were a bit disappointed in St Bart's, as we had been told it was better than Antigua but we didn't think so. We took a taxi ride around the island, collecting our duty free supplies on the way back. Being a French Island we had hoped it would be cheaper, but it was not the case.

17th February 1977. We left St Bart's early in the morning. The weather was calm so we motored all the way to St Martin's arriving midday, having taken three hours. We had enjoyed having a day sail. We had lunch, then went ashore.

We really liked Philipsburg, in the Dutch part of St. Martins. The streets were very clean and well maintained, with no evidence of poverty. There appeared to be more coloured people than at St Bart's where the French appeared to have a policy of not selling land to the Islanders.

On our return to Soñadora we were greeted by two Dominican Islanders, Albert and James trading grapefruit and bananas. It turned out that they knew Joseph who had sailed with us to Dominica. We invited them aboard for a cool soft drink, while we settled a price and traded coffee, tinned powered milk and four seed potatoes with instructions on how to plant and grow them. They would make a change from sweet potatoes and hopefully they would be able to sell them to passing yachties. They seemed keen on the concept though Ron doubted if they would.

We also gave them an address for educational correspondence courses from Oxford University, and also some note paper, envelopes and three books on English, navigation and general science. All in all I think we did a fair exchange. We had enough fresh fruit to last us until we reached Panama and James had the means, as he said 'to better himself.'

All together they visited us for three days, trading and

having good conversation, over a cool drink. I only wished that the British government had done more for Dominica Island than they had appeared to have done. All the Dominicans we had met were well brought up, polite, with a good basic education, thanks in part to Leo's sister Joan who was the school teacher.

Route of Caribbean Cruise

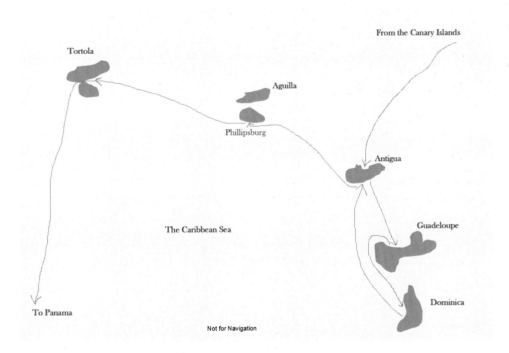

Chapter 16

Back in Antigua

Wwe were looking forward to visiting the Panama Canal. It has quite a history. Back in 1513 the French had discovered a narrow land bridge separating North and South America and the two oceans Atlantic and the Pacific. So France started to construct a sea level canal, but had to stop. The ground was unsuitable and the costs too great, also there was the fear that Nicaraguan volcanoes would explode at anytime. The risk was too much and it was closed down.

In 1903 Columbia (which controlled Panama) refused to allow the USA to build the 'French' canal in Panama, so with the backing of the USA, the people of Panama overthrew the Columbian Government and became independent. This promptly allowed the USA to buy the rights to build the 'French' canal and control the area of build, 48 miles in Panama. The canal was completed in, and first used on August 15th 1914 and is a key contributor to maritime trade. It has been recently enlarged, creating a new lane of traffic along the canal and now the Canal connects 160 countries and 1,700 ports around the world.

The first day at sea was fine, a nice 20 knot wind was pushing us along at a steady 7 knots. We had the awning up over the cockpit and we sat drinking our sundowners thinking we had cracked it at last. Alas, that night the wind went up to force 8 (35 knots) and more as the swell was from the North East and the wind was from the South East. It soon built up to the roughest sea since the Bay of Biscay. We were running under a small working jib poled out and making 10 to 12 knots, shipping the odd sea over the fore and aft decks. These horrendously confused seas were creating 30 to 35 ft waves. They were all coming from different directions and we just couldn't miss them all. Sometimes one would clout us on the side and it felt like we'd hit a brick wall. The Autopilot was still steering better than we could in those confused seas, so we left

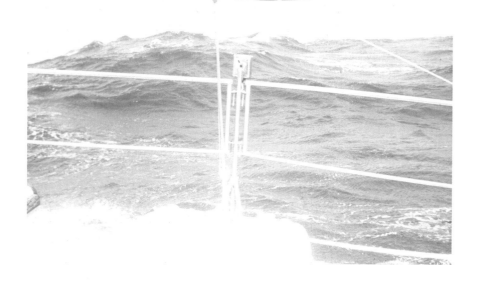

Rough seas on our way to the Panama Canal

it to 'our third crew man.' It is a really marvellous device. Soñadora took it all in her stride. She just shook herself and kept ploughing on averaging 180 miles a day under one little sail. Wonderful!

This weather pattern continued until the last day out from Panama. Ron couldn't get a proper sighting, they were just guesses. Fortunately, on the final day, the wind dropped considerably and Ron was able to get one. He found we had over shot to the North by about 25 miles, so we had a hard beat back against the wind and finally made Panama at midnight on the 7th March 1977. The entrance looked formidable! It was pitch black with no moon to help guide us in, though we did have a very comprehensive chart of the canal and Ron had contacted the Pilot Office and they said that it was OK for us to enter. So in we went, what a nightmare! Lights were flashing everywhere in all colours. Huge ships were going every which way, we just couldn't make head nor tail of where we should be heading. The Captain of one ship leant out of his cockpit cabin looking down on us from a great height, shouted over his rail at us to "get out of the bloody way!" I just smiled and waved to him.

Fortunately, a small motor boat came to our rescue and lead us to the flats, where all visiting yachts were meant to go. We dropped anchor at 12.30am, breathing a sigh of relief, and thanking the chap who had guided us in. About an hour later a launch came alongside with an officer from immigration asking if we wanted to clear now or in the morning. We said "now please." so he came aboard. He was a very friendly American. After he had finished booking us in he warned us about the high rate of crime throughout Panama City and the dangers of travelling inland and not to carry handbags, jewellery, wallets, watches and to be aware of people around us. He was so concerned for our safety he offered that he and his wife would collect us about 11am and take us to the American zone supermarkets to get supplies. We were not really allowed to shop in the American zone, so it was extremely good of him. They arrived as arranged and after our shopping, they came back to lunch on Soñadora. It had been a very interesting and enjoyable morning.

We were quite tired, but still had to row over to the yacht club to book a berth. It was about a half a mile away and yachts were not allowed to use their outboard motors for some reason. As also we would be rowing into the wind so we cheated, Ron pretended to row and I ran the outboard. There was enough ship traffic noise to drown any noise from our little outboard. We thought no-one would know and I am sure we were not the only rule breakers.

The yacht club looked a bit rough, but it ran a 24 hour bar service and a good restaurant, reasonably priced and was very friendly. There was no room on the pontoon which cost £17.50 for 5 days so we had to hang from their buoy, about 30 yards off from the quay. This we were quite happy to do, as it gave us more privacy and we had already done most of our shopping thanks to our American friends and also with the help of a Welshman, John Balson from Swansea who also drove us around and was very helpful. Everyone was looking out for us to make sure we were not attacked. It was very comforting. Mind you, Ron didn't look an easy target, and I had been warned not to carry my handbag or wear any jewellery. Ron said that it would be a brave man who tried to take my purse as being only five foot two, I could bite their knee caps off!

Colon is on the Atlantic Ocean, Caribbean Sea and north side of the canal. It was notorious for its piracy and criminal activities. While we were in Antigua we were told that during the last three years at least 30 yachts had been reported missing, probably attacked. The people on board, were killed and the yacht used for a drug run to America, before being sunk. It was wise not to say when you would be leaving and where you were heading, though it would not be difficult to guess.

The club had recently had a robbery take place on its front walkway. A yachtsman was mugged at midday by four men. They caught three of them which apparently was unusual, but encouraging.

We arranged our transit through the canal for Wednesday 16th March 1977. It cost a total of £75, made up of a measuring fee of £20 which is for the life of the boat, and £23 for the actual transit and £32 for contingences. This would be returned if all went well, which it did. We now had a Panama Transit numbered certificate to be displayed permanently, in the boat's saloon, but costs are much higher now.

To transit the canal you have to have at least five people, on board, four to handle the lines from the yacht to the Panamanian line handlers on the quay. There were two yacht crew on the bows and two on the stern to keep the yacht in the centre chamber of each lock for safety, and a fifth person on the helm as well as the Pilot Captain and his crew of one. We were fortunate that when we were in the Port Captains office arranging our transit we met three Americans, father Joe Noertker and his two sons, Doug and Steve. They were from Osprey, a very attractive 52ft yacht. We arranged to help one another transit through the canal, Soñadora on the 16th at 5am and Osprey on the 17th. at 5am.

The day before we were due to transit the Canal, John Balson our welsh friend came to take me to the market for our last shopping, to post letters, to do the laundry and finally to telephone my Father in the UK. He was recovering from surgery, and reassured me that he was doing well and not to worry, easier said than done.

I loved my Father and as a nurse my first instinct was to jump on a plane home, but I could not leave Ron to cope on his own. He would not have left me if the situation was reversed. At least my Dad had the rest of the family around him, which was a comfort to me.   It is one of the problems of this cruising life that we had debated in full, but really there was no easy answer.   So much depended on where we were, and how safe it was to leave Soñadora.   Panama was definitely not a place to leave anyone, regardless of how exciting and interesting it was.

We returned to find that Ron had taken on fuel and water, and checked the engines. The next leg of our trip was going to be a long one, to the Galapagos and the Marquesas, the French Polynesian Pacific Islands.   It was a good 40 days all told, so getting enough supplies on board was essential, but also good fun when there is plenty to be had. This was not always the case, and we were relatively new to the job of stocking up for long unknown adventures so we had to be careful and thorough. We had quite enjoyed our short stay in Colon and Cristobal, we even went to the cinema and saw a funny western called 'Noon till Three' starring Charles Bronson.

5am Wednesday 16th of March 1977, was our D/ DAY! We would be going from the grey Atlantic to the blue Pacific Ocean.   Our Canal Pilot, Captain Tom Hodgkins arrived with his one crew.   He was a very likable man.   During the day he told me that he was divorced and had two young daughters. He had been in the Canal Zone for 22 months. He liked the job, but not the then system.

Joe and his boys arrived. It was a really fine morning, Tom our pilot took the helm while his partner gathered us together to talk us through the handling of the lines and the routine to take us safely through the canals.   It was all very exciting.   So off we went arriving at the first lock on time, only to be told we would have to wait an hour for our ship, Seaservice of Monrovia to arrive.   So I went to the galley to make breakfast for us all while the men made Soñadora secure and Tom checked that we all knew how to handle the lines, hauling in the slack or letting them out to keep her steady in the centre chamber and to pull them in quickly when he told them

Seaservice Monrovia arriving and Tom indicating to 'follow that ship'

to do so. We didn't want them fouling the propellers of either Soñadora or the ship.

We had just finished breakfast when our ship arrived, manoeuvring just ahead of Soñadora as the huge gates closed silently astern of us. The water started to rush in from the 8ft diameter holes in the floor of the lock taking 8 minutes to fill, the linesmen were kept very busy hauling in the slack to keep Soñadora centrally steady. With the turbulence of the water rushing in and the rotation of Monrovia's ship propellers, if the lines are not kept taught damage to a yacht can occur. As soon as the lock was full the forward gates were opened and with the help of the mules (electric locomotives) up on the quay the ship was moved into the next chamber and we followed behind. Twice more the whole routine was repeated, and then we came out upon the broad waters of the Canal Zone of the GATUN LAKE 85ft above sea level and 23 miles long.

We had had a very pleasant and interesting motor sail across the lakes to the down locks. It was a bit spooky as there were dead decaying trees poking up through the water everywhere, they looked like head stones in a grave yard, which I suppose in a

Panama Canal 16th March 1977, last 3 locks going down to the Pacific
Ocean and Balboa Yacht club to Port

This picture is Showing the
depth of an empty lock and
the electric locomotives
(mule trains) which pull the
ships into the locks

Port and starboard exits from the Canal into the Pacific Ocean

Seaservice of Monrovia can be seen leaving well ahead of us

Looking back to the Canal entrance and exits from the Pacific Ocean

way they were. We had no photos of this as sadly they had been stolen, while in the post. We were told that it was for the stamps. Consequently, I didn't post anymore letters until we got to New Zealand.

When we got to the down locks we had to tie up to a tug and go down with it. Our ship Seaservice of Monrovia can be seen leaving well ahead of us.

Coming out of the Canal, passing under the Thatcher Ferry Bridge, Captain Tom had warned us about the tremendous strength of the incoming tide, yachts had to be able to maintain 5 knots, against the tide and were not allowed to drop an anchor or use their dinghy's, we had to tie up to the yacht clubs extra strong buoys. Once we had got safely buoyed, we had lunch. Tom said it was the best lunch he had had on a yacht in transit, and we said he was the best Pilot Captain! Mutual admiration society was in full swing.

We now had to catch the train back to Cristobal to help bring Joe's yacht Osprey through the Canal for the 5am transit the next day. Making sure Soñadora was safe and closed up for the night, we hailed the yacht clubs water taxi to get ashore. Ron and Joe booked in at the Panama yacht club, which was very friendly, reassuring us that Soñadora would be quite safe with them, they ordered a taxi to take us all to the train station.

At that time all yachts had to transit the canal behind a ship. This could be a very frightening experience. Especially if the captain forgets he has a yacht travelling behind his ship and revs up. The back wash from the ships propellers had damaged many yachts for instance, only the previous week a New Zealand yacht had had its cleats and stanchions torn right out of its deck from the turbulence of the ships propellers pulling on the ropes. Fortunately, these days' yachts go through with other yachts, not big ships. We had, had a very enjoyable time onboard Osprey with Joe and his

Looking back at the Thatcher Ferry Bridge

family and it was good to go through the canal again. You do see more the second time around.

We stayed a week at Balboa Yacht club. There was so much to explore in Panama City, a very busy, noisy, crowded, but fascinating place, we were advised by the club to use taxis they were so cheap and safer when visiting the city. The public transport service was not very reliable.

Now was the time to move on, after a successful and enjoyable trip through the Panama Canal. We left Balboa in the morning of 23rd March 1977 full to the brim with diesel, water and supplies and motored out into the misty, windless, Gulf of Panama and the lovely blue waters of the Pacific Ocean. We were bound for the Galapagos and the Marquesas group of islands and beyond. All quite different from the grey seas of the Atlantic Ocean.

We reflected on our journey so far and were happy and well satisfied with the first part of our sail around the world.

Caribbean to Panama and the Pacific

Leaving the misty waters of the Gulf of Panama

Carole saying Hello to the Dolphins in the blue waters of the Pacific

Chapter 17   Caribbean to Panama and the Pacific

As if to welcome us to the Pacific Ocean we were being escorted by a large pod of Dolphins surrounding us, and a flock of Pelicans flying low over the rolling waves above us, they must have all been chasing a shoal of fish, as well as piloting us. What a delightful sight it was. Our convoy stayed with us all morning, just magic, and a good omen for our continued adventure through the Pacific and its beautiful islands, described and illustrated in Book 2.

Includes the following Chapters:-

Galapagos The Mysterious Islands

The Beautiful Marquesas Islands

Coral Islands   Tuamotu Coral Islands

Passengers to Tahiti

Moorea the most Beautiful of all

Raitea Tahaa

Bora Bora   Bastille Celebrations

Pearls and Fruit Juice, Rewriting, The Cook Islands

"Niue" The Savage Island

Tonga Vivau, The Friendly Islands

Fiji

Christmas in New Zealand

The Tasman See Storms, Jam and a One Legged Hitchhiker to Sydney

Cruising the Barrier Reef to Thursday Island

Darwin after the Hurricane

Christmas in Perth